Radical Innovation

Steinar Wasa Tverlid

Radical Innovation

Everybody can if they know how

Copyright © 2020 by
Vigmostad & Bjørke AS
All Rights Reserved

First Edition / Printing 1
ISBN: 978-82-450-3377-9
Graphic production: John Grieg, Bergen

Enquiries about this text can be directed to:
Fagbokforlaget
Kanalveien 51
5068 Bergen
Tel.: 55 38 88 00
email: fagbokforlaget@fagbokforlaget.no
www.fagbokforlaget.no

All rights reserved. No part of this publication may be reproduced, stored in a retrieval system, or transmitted, in any form or by any means, electronic, mechanical, photo-copying, recording, or otherwise, without the prior written permission of the publisher.

Preface

Basis for the book

Have you ever felt the urge to advance faster than the pace you see around you? Have you ever felt impatient about things you would like to improve, from those small everyday matters to those large challenges mankind is facing, but what you see around you is moving so slowly? I certainly have, and I am doing something about it. This is my story.

For my entire life I have been overly interested in how things work, how we can make them work better and how we can make them last longer. My first paid job was handling customers in a petrol station providing them fuel and other services as the only person on site – at the age of 14. My choice of studies was quite obvious, mechanical engineering, which ultimately brought me to a Ph.D. in material science, while driving a bus in my spare time and a truck during holidays. During my entire professional career, I have had technical positions in three multi-national industrial companies: Hydro Aluminium, Hydro Oil and Energy, and presently Equinor (which was Statoil before 2018). It is not an overstatement to say that my contributions up until recently have had a strong technical focus.

My passion for mechanical systems has also had some peculiar effects privately. I held on to the car I bought as a student until it was sold recently, more than 20 years later of daily use. By this time, the car had a mileage equivalent of more than 14 times around equator, only receiving maintenance by others on a couple of occasions. Perhaps it is fair to say that I am interested in technical matters more than the average person.

This interest, in combination with experience from various positions in three rather different multi-national companies, has given me the opportunity to see improvement points along my way, to an extent that patterns and vital mechanisms in the innovation process itself started to emerge. This led to many new concept suggestions, successful and by all means failing tests, a vast number of patent applications and eventually also quite a few patents – implementations as well.

However, it has also brought me a lot of frustration, more frustration than one would think. There is a world of difference between ideation and innovation. Proposing a well described concept could mean the end of ideation, but you are nowhere near an innovation at this point. To qualify as innovation, a new idea is not enough – the concept needs to be implemented and also create value. This normally involves significant funding, complicated qualification processes and facing many people who may not see the world through the same lens as the inventor, which is certainly the case in large companies but also to an extent for smaller companies and start-ups.

Frustration, even lots of frustration, can be positive if the internal energy it generates can be channeled in the right direction. I must somehow, more or less consciously, have managed to find this golden path, because as a direct consequence of venting this frustration out on the research director in Equinor, together with some improvement proposals I had, I was given the opportunity to build a radical innovation muscle; a formal pure radical innovation effort with creative meetings on a regular basis. Literally overnight I went from having just any position to having the best position in the entire company, at least to my opinion.

And not just in any company. Equinor has for quite some time been the largest company in the Nordic countries. The company is generally known to be a front runner in innovation within the energy sector and was even rated number seven on Fortune's lists of the most innovative companies in the world in 2011 – all sectors included. Equinor was also on Forbes' top ten innovative company list around the same time. However, I still felt that there was a significant improvement potential if systems could be put in place to make valuable radical innovation a reliable product from regular efforts rather than more coincidental opportunities or even worse a result of the stars being favorably placed astrologically. I later discovered that systematic radical innovation processes in parallel to normal improvement processes is referred to as ambidexterity in innovation leadership theory.

The formal radical innovation group was a unique chance to try out some ideas on virtual teams that I had mentally developed over time. Virtual in this context means a regular and time limited sub structure occasionally forming within and even across the formal organization. During this work I had my suspicions confirmed; what a tremendously powerful force radical innovation can be in a company, if it is done more or less correctly – the model is in fact quite robust. This force goes way beyond the radical concepts, it goes beyond the radical team and those involved in making those radical concepts become reality. It can affect the majority of the employees, it doesn't have to take a long time like major changes almost always do, and the best of all, it could be really cheap. However, the radical effort can equally easily be a flop that creates frustration and dissent if handled in a poor way.

About a year after kicking off systematic work on radical innovation, the same research director gave innovation a significant facelift in the company through a number of changes, including the introduction of a dedicated innovation team with corporate responsibility. I got to join the innovation team and at the point of writing this, I am still a member of this team. The team built a structure and knowledge foundation also based on innovation principles arising from my radical innovation groups, an effort which was continued and expanded in the time to follow. The same innovation principles have later been transferred to and offered in the form of workshops around the company and even agile project management tools.

This book is a practical guide to innovation that builds on this entire journey, from my very first experiences with innovation over several decades, via the point where I was given the exceptional opportunity to be a part of building systematic radical innovation abilities, through all the important learning in building the present radical innovation structure to some further improvement points not yet implemented.

I am a dreamer. I guess we are all dreamers in one way or another. Some of my dreams turned out to be within reach and I could pursue them – so I did – over and over again, extending that reach.

My motivation with this book is to share my knowledge from this journey so that many more can have the opportunity to pursue their dreams to benefit themselves, their surroundings and preferably to everyone unleashing that tremendous satisfaction of making a positive difference.

Follow your dreams. Everybody can if they know how!

Thanks

However, before I go into details, I would sincerely like to thank a number of people who have helped me in different ways to materialize the content between these two covers.

Firstly, I would like to thank my family for keeping up with disproportionate amounts of innovation matters, therein all the crazy ideas that need testing. Sincere thanks to the entire innovation team in Equinor for their support making this story what it is today and in particular Jan Richard Sagli, Reda Rezzoug, Bjørn Kåre Viken and Tor Ulleberg for their direct help in the publishing process. I would also like to include the R&D team in Hydro Aluminium Extrusion for inspiration during the making of the necessary foundation upon which this story could be built, especially the amazing Richard Dickson.

The talented Erik Nijveld, CEO and founder of Deployment Matters deserves a deep bow for many good discussions and for high quality feedback on the current project. Also, the feedback from Elinor Falkmann and Truls Berg was highly appreciated and helped to uplift the story to what it is now.

It goes without saying that I want to thank all those who have been members of my Radical Innovation team over the years, from whom I have learned so much, as well as those invited for just a few sessions helping us improve quality at the dispense of nonsense. Also belonging to this group is the deeply innovation-engaged Ingunn Johanne Ness, who followed our group over approximately two years at the same time as she was a Ph.D.

student from University of Bergen, and has contributed to this story on many levels, including a dedicated appendix section in this book.

Last but certainly not least I would like to direct special gratitude to Karl Johnny Hersvik, the former research director in Equinor, who strongly believed in innovation as a key for success, who understood the overall objectives of my plans and gave me a green light to start the first radical innovation pilot back in 2011. The same special gratitude goes to my first group member (and in the beginning the only other member), Jone Torsvik, who has stood firmly shoulder-to-shoulder with me through ups and downs all the way... and still does. He happens to be one of those few "borne to create and innovate."

As they read through this entire story, I hope all of those mentioned here feel that a part of this journey also belongs to them!

Contents

Introduction – why radical innovation	12
Misconceptions killing your ability to actively control your future	21
Who takes value from this book	22
This book in a few words	26
Get started – form a radical innovation group	34
Build a group and a meeting structure	36
Implement efficient innovation work methods that yield radical results	58
What works and what does not in a radical innovation group	84
Integrate – fit innovation groups into your organization	106
Build a network of radical innovation groups	108
Build a direct communication channel to the leadership	118
Radical innovation as workshops for non-skilled	128
Radical innovation to assure agility in project-based work	134
Implement – take out the full value potential	148
Radical innovation not only for tomorrow but also today	153
Dual interdependency – the best of both worlds	166
Incentives and culture – make sustainable growth	170
Incentives promoting cooperation	173
Building a sustainable innovation culture for growth	182
Appendix A: Academic perspective by Dr. Ingunn Johanne Ness	196
The Equinor radical innovation pilot group – a case in a Ph.D. project on interdisciplinary innovation work	197
Terms and expressions	208
References	212
Index	216

Introduction – why radical innovation

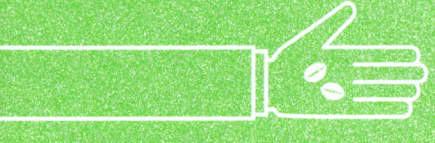

Chapter summary

This chapter is an introduction to what this book can offer the readers. It is about differentiating between incremental and radical innovation, about taking both of them seriously, but the focus is on the radical side, which is where most companies fail. This chapter ends with a bullet overview about what the book offers the readers; a complete guide on how to build a well working radical innovation muscle.

In this chapter you will hear more about the following.
- The importance of taking a systematic approach to radical innovation, and that only applying parts of the entire model will help significantly
- Incremental innovation, which is improving today's solutions by building further on the knowledge associated to that solution
- Radical innovation being a new direction compared to today's solutions and, as such, replacing current knowledge with new
- Misconceptions associated with radical innovation
- The typical reader of this book, and that although the model is built on a company structure, the main parts can be valuable for smaller informal groups and even single people

Portfolio example

Down hole milling center

After changing from the metal forming industry to the oil and energy sector, I was a bit surprised about the way metal was removed down in oil or gas wells when, for example, a part of the metal casing needed to be removed for whatever reason. The way this was done at the time was to bull head the way through the part that was to be removed. This was of course a terrible burden on the equipment. The bull head was therefore usually made of sharp pieces of the dead-hard material tungsten carbide baked into a matrix, whose task was to keep these almost diamond hard particles from detaching as long as possible during the brutal fight between the no longer wanted high quality steel and the demolishing bull head. As if to make the conditions even tougher, the bull head's first firm fixture was the rotating top drive on the drilling rig, perhaps several hundred and even thousands of meters away from the milling action. The bull head and top drive was connected via a drill pipe, which under such distances would act very similarly to a spring torqueing up and releasing energy as the system sticks and slips. This generates significant vibrations, which again makes the local milling action where a cutting edge slices off a chip of the work piece highly varying and really unpredictable. During my time in the metal forming industry, I was the manufacturing manager of a factory with a number of machining centers amongst them a few CNC milling machines. In our efforts to improve the performance of these machines, I learned some basics about machining. Somewhat simplified one can say that the best cutting conditions are achieved when each cutting edge of the mill cuts an optimal volume of metal with the right shape for every cut. The parameters to control were the cutting depth, speed and mill rotations per minute, which would define the volume and shape of each cut. However, one effect has the potential to destroy even the best set of parameters – vibrations. The more the mill vibrates, the more discrepancy between the intended and real cutting conditions. So, what you typically see is that when the vibrations are under control, the milled surface is smoother, the milling job is faster, the precision of the cut is higher and the wear of the tool is lower, often significantly.

Then back to the traditional down hole milling process. I would argue that this type of milling might as well be called a major vibration generator, diametrically opposite of what you need to get decent milling conditions. This is also clearly reflected in the results of traditional milling. The duration of similar drilling jobs varied a lot. The debris ranged from powder to big lumps of steel. The bull head tool could last for a while, but could also be destroyed in a very short time, accompanied by frequent stuck situations. Major well cleaning sessions after milling was also common. With experience from modern CNC milling machines, I kicked off a project I called "From Sledgehammer to Science" and looked at how we could apply CNC milling principles down hole in order to improve performance accordingly. This resulted in Patent Publication No. WO/2010/066276 Wellbore Machining Device (see Figure 1). I promoted this internally and this was generally well received, but not well enough for anyone to step up and commit time and recourses to get the project running. Within our potential user segment in the company (in other words those holding the business need), we had experts on traditional milling, but held limited experience on modern machining center type of milling. After all, tool making is not a part of my company's business model – we use tools, we don't make them. The internal recommendation was to propose this idea to the service companies who performed those types of milling jobs for us; so I did. I proposed this to the company contacts for one company performing this type of jobs for us, and soon I found myself on an international flight with an invitation in my pocket for a meeting with the CEO himself.

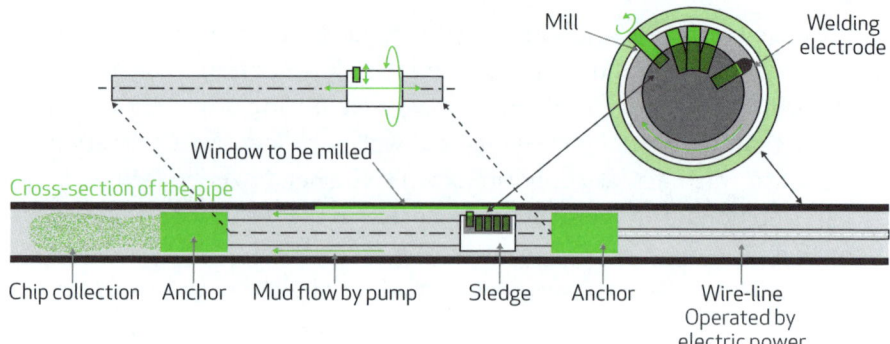

Figure 1   The down hole milling concept in principle sketches.

> The CEO and his team showed great interest in the technology and in our company's eagerness to get this realized. The latter part of the interest was fortified by the commercial discussion that, to my opinion, demonstrated for the service company that we were not too eager to push this new technology unless the service company saw the potential in this themselves. I don't know what they discussed before and after we were in that meeting, but the effort faded slowly away. What I can say is that a service company selling tools and hours using those tools on-site might not be too eager to develop a new technology that will eliminate all specialized tools to the benefit of one universal tool that has the capacity to cut the operational time down to a fraction of traditional operations.

This is one amongst several stories that made me understand that a company needs to take responsibility for its own progress. We are the closest to our own business needs and should be in the best position to assess the best remedy for those needs. So instead of sharing those needs and leaving development entirely up to other companies whose business side of the need may not exactly coincide with ours, a company should instead take responsibility for innovation itself – at least the early phase ideation and stay on long enough for the project to build enough inertia to either be finished or be stopped because of arguments adapted to the original need of the end customer.

A part of the story above is that the milling technology has slowly and steadily moved towards vibration and chip control, although there is quite a bit left before we have effective down hole CNC machining. We lost many years of steeper progress because we were not able to develop a promising radical concept with the ability to jump many small expensive development steps. As a result, I dedicated much of my time building systematic radical innovation capacity in the company – a story I intend to share in this book.

More about...

...what radical innovation is and how it stands out from incremental innovation, and how innovation relates to LEAN and standardization. We normally distinguish between two types of innovation: incremental and radical innovation.

Incremental innovation

Incremental innovation, often also referred to as routine innovation, is about further developing the solutions at hand. It is a part of continuous improvement efforts, which enhance the performance without introducing a new direction. Fundamentally, one can say that the new knowledge acquired builds on the knowledge associated with the existing solution. As such, one can argue that this is linear development (see Figure 2). An example can be the next model of a BMW, where it sometimes can be difficult to pinpoint the exact changes apart from the price increase, on both the visible level and the invisible. In this case, the new model definitely builds on the knowledge of the previous, and does not represent a change of direction.

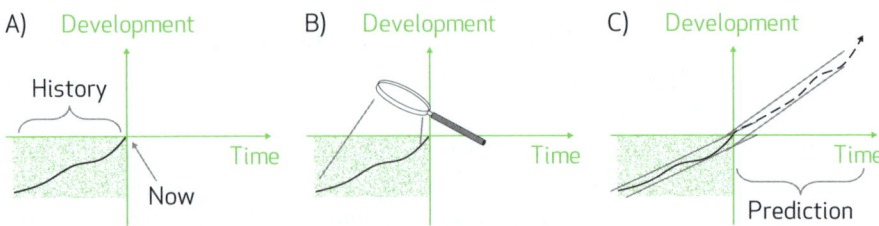

Figure 2 Illustration of the development with time for Incremental Innovation. Due to the linear character, one can use the past (A), study what has been (B) and make predictions about future developments (C) with an associated risk.

Radical and disruptive innovation

Radical innovation is breaking with the development pattern of the present solution and finding a completely new direction (see Figure 3). In this case, the knowledge required for the new solution also breaks with the knowledge associated with the previous solution, rendering the latter knowledge obsolete. This is often also referred to as lateral thinking. An example of this is the tractor replacing horses in farming. The knowledge base forming the foundation for manufacturing and use of tractors is totally different from that associated to horses.

A closely related term is disruptive innovation, which is normally used for new business model directions, while radical then refers more to technical innovation. For simplicity, in the following, radical innovation will be used for both technical and business model innovation, and indicate all innovation representing a completely new direction.

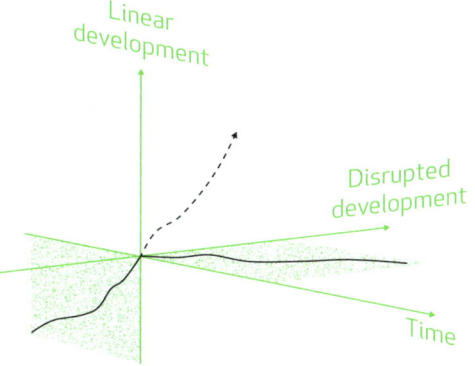

Figure 3   Illustration of a development that is disrupted (or a radical new solution has been introduced). The expected linear development (the dashed line) did not occur, but took a new direction along a totally new axis (the black line after origo).

So, what might then be the connection between innovation and continuous improvement tools like the LEAN processes in which standardization is an integral part? In order to understand this, it might be useful to consider the different development steps of a successful technology, from the time somebody understands that this is a need people would be willing to pay for until this product is the standard solution, which then forms the basis for any further improvement and a possible next solution. An example of these steps is illustrated in Figure 4.

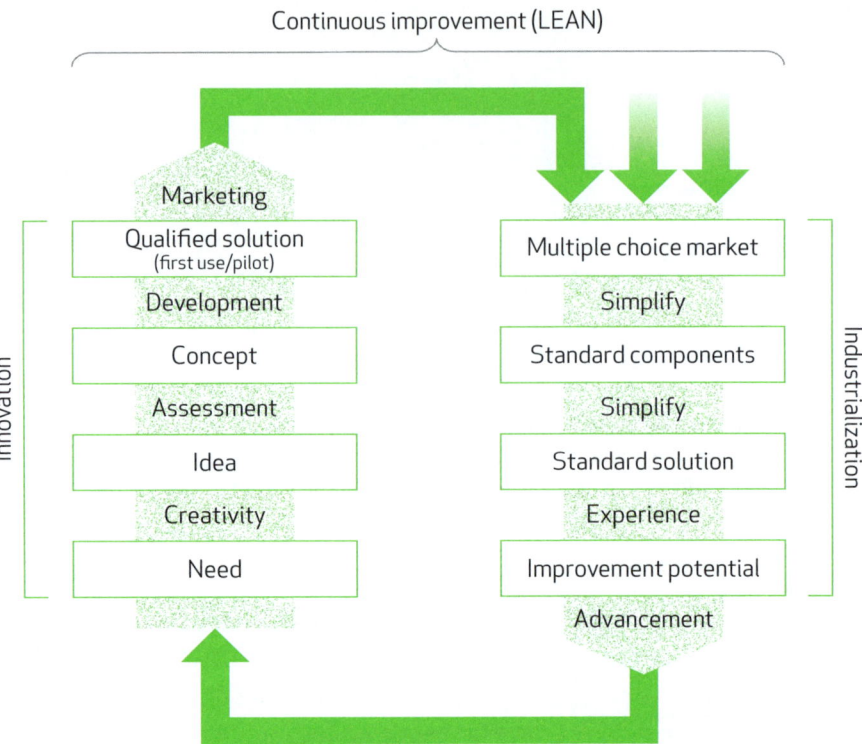

Figure 4   An example of a continuous improvement cycle including the divergent innovation side (left) and the convergant industrialization side (right).

The continuous improvement process consists of two principally different processes, developing new solutions which cover a need. As soon as the new solution is applied and creates value, this is innovation, since it covers the three main elements of innovation: *new*, *valuable* and *implemented* (see page 208). This is the diverging part of the continuous improvement process, illustrated as the left side of Figure 4. If the product needs further development, the left side needs to be repeated. When the product is good enough, it is introduced to the market and starts competing with other equivalent products as it moves into the converging part of the process on the right side of Figure 4. Here the focus is increased production efficiency. This is about eliminating waste, solution simplification and standardizing components or solutions to release value through mass production and limit storage cost, all of which is about taking something away. This can indeed be *valuable* and it may well be *implemented* too, but removing elements lacks the "*new*" component and is therefore not innovation. I would rather call this *industrialization* as it optimizes mass production, minimum inventory and reduced transport, or simply increases efficiency. On the other hand, one could always say that increased efficiency could be achieved by improving the product with new updated features, but then you are divergent and move over to the left side of Figure 4.

In order to improve you might innovate something new or perform your present tasks more efficiently, all of which is continuous improvement such as the LEAN process if this is done systematically over time.

Misconceptions killing your ability to actively control your future

Most people think that radical innovation is a coincidental process where alertly waiting, luck and even magic are what it takes to succeed. Considering that radical innovation is the basis for active and targeted strategy work which potentially provide companies clear, visual and communicative options for the future, it is way too important to leave to coincidence. The good news is that radical innovation can systematically be produced over and over again with relatively simple means if you know what to do. And better yet, one of the best ways is also really cheap and efficient. It is like a tourist class plane ticket gets you to your destination before the first class passengers.

Here are some other common misconceptions associated radical innovation with a reference to where they are addressed in this book.

- Innovation/ideation doesn't lead to anything but useless wild ideas (*see INTEGRATE – FIT INNOVATION GROUPS INTO YOUR ORGANIZATION on page 106*).
- If radical innovation leads to something, it is certainly nowhere near what we were looking for (*see for example More about on page 56 and Figure 35 on page 167 with associated explanations*).
- Radical innovation is too risky. It is better to rely on incremental innovation, which is the low risk version of innovation. This will bring us safely to the radical level eventually (*see More about on page 23*).
- Radical ideation can be done, but implementation won't happen anyway. The organization is not capable of adaptation (*see IMPLEMENT – TAKE OUT THE FULL VALUE POTENTIAL on page 148*).
- With radical innovation only those "radical oddballs" with no practical insight are going to shape our future (*see Build a network of radical innovation groups on page 108*).
- Innovation is too expensive (*see GET STARTED – FORM A RADICAL INNOVATION GROUP on page 34*).
- Radical innovation is about new directions for the company. This work is for top management and the strategy department, and no one else (*see Figure 22 on page 110 with associated explanations*).
- Strategy work is mainly about how we advance relative to our competitors. Therefore, external focus, input and even assistance are as fundamental if not more important than internal focus to achieve a viable strategy (*see More about on page 29 and Building an innovative culture amongst the Passive Users on page 191*).
- We have tried these things before. It simply doesn't work. But we are still around, so what's the point? (*read the entire book, please*).

Who takes value from this book

This book aims to motivate those who need advancement or simply those who would like to positively influence progress proactively through innovation. The most obvious reader is a leader in a medium to large company who cannot afford expensive programs and does not have as a default the luxury to enjoy a Silicon Valley type of innovation culture. Managers squeezed between profit demand and an increased pace on competitor products would indeed also find the time spent between these two covers useful. Team leaders and project managers who feel their projects needs renewal, especially if earlier efforts have had limited effect, should not put the book away before the section with workshop tips are carefully undertaken. Core readers might well be impatient employees who feel progress is too slow and their ideas are constantly being batted down (like myself). Then you will soon also know which book to buy for your boss for Christmas. But perhaps the largest effect can be expected from single freelance dreamers who simply are tired of waiting for the more established business community to move on those screaming needs you see around you and would like a share of the value this could offer. Common to all of the proactive innovation contributors above is the need for a practical, simple and cheap tool to advance each respective endeavor. That is exactly what this book offers.

More about...

...**the connection between advancement and effort during development (the S-curve) and how to "outperform evolution".**
Looking at how the world has evolved since life came to earth, progress has followed incremental principles. Evolution is incremental. The development of species has taken place in very small steps between generations. The changes are so small that many generations are necessary to spot real differences. This is clearly incremental in the sense that the main direction is maintained and the changes are small improvements. If the change didn't represent an improvement, the branch of this particular species would soon die out and the stronger branch would survive. Therefore, every small increment must be an improvement in evolutional perspective, similar to the principals behind continuous improvement of products, processes, procedures and services within companies.

If evolution follows incremental principles, why should a company divert from this well-established practice and do something as risky as radical innovation? And why is it so difficult for companies to grab radical opportunities even if they know renewal is needed, like the case of Kodak. Kodak was not able to embrace digitalization of images before it was too late and chose to stay with what they knew the best: classic film technology. Some of the answer can be found in the "S" curve for technology development, for example as elaborated by Clayton M Christensen[16] (see Figure 5a). The x-axis is applied effort (cumulative), while the y-axis is advancement. In this context, the life cycle of a technology will typically make up an S-curve; after a slow start in the emerging phase where much effort is needed to get the product going, there will come a phase with rapid development with moderate effort. When the technology reaches the mature stage, much more effort is needed to advance the technology. At this point it takes radical innovation to maintain the advancement pace without disproportionate effort. A new technology (or business model) with a higher long-term potential is needed to advance significantly. The fundamental challenge is that the new technology often starts off at a lower advancement (or efficiency) level than the old mature technology. But the real value may still be significantly higher due to higher growth *potential*. Contrary to incremental innovation, an intermediate dip in efficiency must be expected when choosing the radical innovation track. For example, when the first tractors came and challenged the traditional horse as the main power source for farmers, it took many years before the tractor was the clear choice compared to the horse on a task-to-task consideration when it came to efficiency. The first tractors were slow, heavy, unstable in off-road terrain, dangerous, not user friendly and not particularly strong. Today we know that no horse would stand a chance against the tractor. To sacrifice some efficiency a while for a growth potential is very difficult for many, and totally impossible for evolution. Those of us who have driven a car with manual gear box know this dilemma. Changing gear during acceleration will intermediately reduce the power before the engine yet again reaches maximum effect. Evolution would not change to second gear. Would you?

The advancement space between the end of one S-curve and the beginning of the next, the efficiency drop, is a major barrier for radical solutions, particularly for large companies. It is indeed controversial to invest money in something that may yield value at one point far into the future, which then may even threaten well-working beneficial products of today, and, on top of this, has a poorer performance than today's product at present. This book will propose a method to make the radical changes easier to promote.

Evolution would not change to second gear.

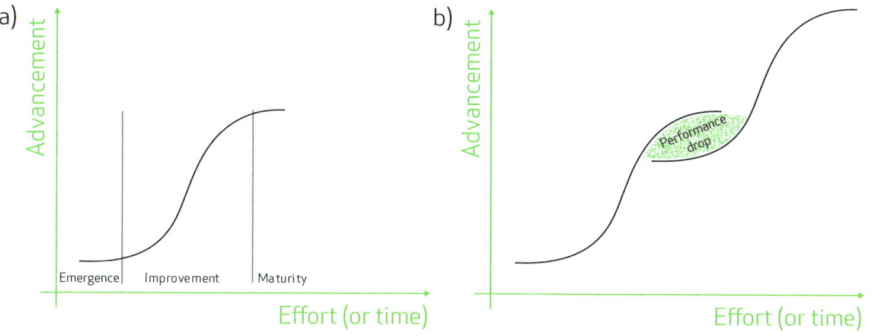

Figure 5   The "S"-curve of technology development: a) for one technology from the Emerging phase, through Rapid Development and Declining Improvement to Maturity, b) A radical innovation offering a higher growth potential, but starts with a drop in performance compared to existing technology from a).

This book in a few words

I have spent about two decades working deeply into the subject of this book from various perspectives in large companies and building this capacity on a daily basis. This stands out from the vast majority of innovation books where the writer(s) have studied a number of companies, successful and/or not successful, sharing insight based on statistical analyses from an external perspective.

The book at hand sums up the knowledge from this journey in a story-like format. It is meant to be a handbook for the generation of radical innovation. The step-by-step method allows a company to almost organically reproduce radical concepts while keeping the budget at a really reasonable level. The effort will remain modest while the effect, on the contrary, will soon be quite visible throughout the company and beyond. The consequence will not only be a clearer vision about alternative long-term future predictions, but will also allow this insight to guide present decisions in order to proactively align with what is already coming now. Deliberate and targeted use of mental anchors placed in future scenarios at the right moment are essential for bringing everybody on board with this mission.

This is most certainly *not the only way to be innovative*, neither incrementally nor radically. There are numerous ways to renew. The only real failure is not trying. The story shared within these pages, I believe is practical due to its scalability, overall involvement, low cost and effort, and its productivity. It is simply worth sharing.

The main lines are the following.

1. Build radical innovation engines as virtual teams around the company and feed them with contemporary business needs.

    a. Group members are chosen according to certain personal skills and qualities (but these are not as strict as one would think).
    b. Each member remains for the most part a resource in his/her unit and participates in the radical innovation work perhaps about ten percent of his/her time, apart from one organizer who spends some more time.

c   The group meets physically on a regular basis within the ten percent set aside for radical work.
   d   The group is fed with business needs (from the leadership, strategy, themselves or others).

2 Leave the group to work out radical concepts.

   a   The group follows a certain procedure to develop radical concepts with viable business potentials (business cases) with a long-time perspective.
   b   The group will convince themselves and later also others by performing little and simple "showstopper" tests funding themselves from their own small budget.
   c   Concepts considered promising will be presented in a visual manner by the organizer to a representative with strategy responsibility in the company leadership.

3 Involve those who are not members of regular virtual radical innovation teams in workshops based on the same fundamental method to participate in the future outlook effort.
4 The different radical concepts will make up a set of alternative routes for the company leadership to make sound decisions on.

   a   The company leadership (or strategy team) will put up different future scenarios filled with content from the radical groups but also normal company strategy considerations and, as is in the mandate for leadership, they will lead the way.
   b   The preferred scenario (or concrete radical concept) can now take two somewhat different routes based on projected value considerations.

       i   Start realizing the scenario through a new development program.
       ii   Feed the scenario back into relevant parts of the organization as guides to achieve immediate effects through a higher stretch in

ongoing incremental innovation efforts (by moving their mental anchors into the future).

Route i:
A careful and critical development work is started to see if the proposed future scenario or a concrete radical concept is feasible as presented with the anticipated value. Even if this process is fast tracked, these are normally long-term projects.

Route ii:
The scenario or concept is rerouted back into the organization to create benefit in a short-term perspective by motivating the rest of the organization to stretch. The direct benefit of this is that all incremental projects are likely to increase the innovation pace at the same time as, more indirectly, the organizations innovation culture is strengthened. This option is the best of both worlds; it offers short-term result, short-term value and the low risk through frequent customer feed-back in the nature of incremental innovation, at the same time as it offers the targeted development pace, competitiveness, and the high reward of radical innovation.

5. Apply these principles in project management to assure adaptability to external and internal changes in an agile way while maintaining alignment in the organization.

Each of these steps will be described in detail in the coming chapters sharing practical experience and useful advice.

More about...

...companies' more or less subconscious preference to incremental innovation and failing ability to systematically produce radical innovation.
Company executives, particularly in larger companies, face a tough dilemma on daily basis; On one hand they need to be attractive for investors. It's about the value of the company, which again is linked to its creditor rating and ability to grow. Investors generally like to reduce risk and prefer predictable, often short-term benefit[4], quite opposite to what radical innovation is known to offer (although this book tries to challenge that). As such, investors have a tendency to avoid companies with a significant budget for radical innovation.

On the other hand, all companies need to renew themselves. Innovation pace is increasing. Some even claim this increase is exponential[27]. Small agile companies and start-ups adapt faster to a changing world where old opportunities are replaced by brand new ones pointing in a completely different direction.

The dilemma of being seen as not investing thoroughly in radical innovation and the need to constantly renew oneself makes things difficult for leadership. A typical result is focus on incremental innovation rather than radical. Incremental innovation is generally more predictable, associated with lower risk, constant improvement (no performance dip – see More about on page 23) and faster payback being a fairly predictable ratio of the investment. There is always a way you can improve your product, service and business model, if only just marginally. And marginal changes are inherently quicker to implement. Many times, it is even beneficial to split a transition of a product or a service into many small steps distributed over time in order to constantly offer new versions of the product or the service, which, indirectly, makes the previous versions outdated and old fashioned. New models of cars are an example thereof, with constantly small improvements for every new model. These may increase sales, and as such both sales and development are attended to, as long as the customers do not prefer a competitor with a faster pace.

If a company does not invest in radical innovation, by constantly challenging itself on whether the existing product/service will also be the best direction to go in the future and questioning itself whether there are other better ways to cover the need (or new needs to address), the market can suddenly be lost to someone else finding that new way first. For example, it doesn't really matter how brilliant your keys are if you have developed over time the world's best key panel for phones, now that the touch screen came and took over that market.

Neither efficiency nor quality can make up for wrong direction.

That being said, incremental innovation is and will remain the backbone of global progress. The incremental to radical innovation ratio when it comes to resource distribution should be way in favor of incremental innovation (perhaps somewhere in the range of ten-to-one for a medium to large company, just to mention a number) depending on the segment, of course. Improvement of existing products, services and business model is and should be the major part of global progress. The world would not be the same if we would still drive around in our Model T Fords waiting for a radically new means of individual transport to be launched. However, it may prove detrimental to focus *only* on the incremental part of innovation, which too many do. Radical innovation is often left undone, or rather left to coincidence. There could be many reasons for this, one of them being the fear of falling investor interest, as discussed above. A second reason could be the lack of patience and confidence that the radical effort eventually will yield results. A third reason could be focus on short-term cash perhaps accompanied by a hope or even solid trust that the company can buy its way out of this dilemma through acquisitions when something attractively new comes up. A fourth reason may be the belief that interesting concepts will come from somewhere in due time if the potential is there, and there is nothing one can do to speed the process anyway. Yet a fifth could be that a company tries, but it doesn't yield results. The most common reason may well be that upper management fears losing tight control anywhere since the reputation of radical innovation is perceived to be unpredictable in nature from A to Z. Whichever reason is the dominant, it seems most companies, particularly large ones, are under-performing when it comes to radical innovation. It also seems if one does not make a particular effort, systematic innovation will be limited to incremental only.

Some companies decide to outsource radical innovation, paying other companies or consultants to help map the future options. This is indeed better than doing nothing and may also be a positive contribution to a thorough internal process. However, if the external view is dominant, the following could be useful to consider.

1. The external part may well be speaking to all your competitors, providing them similar recommendations, recommendations that may well be built on insight from the work with you.
2. An important part of success is to leverage the internal competence and culture in the best possible way, both at present and in the future. Externals may not be in the best position to judge internal qualities.
3. Radical innovation is not an occasional activity, but permanent, systematic hard work.
4. The "not invented here" syndrome affects your ability to succeed[3]. A self-developed solution with a companywide involvement level from cradle to implementation/production has a far higher probability to be successful than a solution "imposed" onto key stakeholders in your organization from someone else.
5. Not only does radical innovation work require knowledge, but it also raises the knowledge base further through the process. This knowledge is important to build a platform for long-term profitability. It is indeed a pity to send all this competence out of the door when the report is handed over.

6   Innovation work is constantly building innovation culture (see *INCENTIVES AND CULTURE – MAKE SUSTAINABLE GROWTH*, page 170). Progress on radical innovation will positively influence the overall innovation culture, which benefits the incremental as well. By using externals, one may miss out on the full culture building potential.

If internal radical innovation for whatever reason is not an option and your company never gets to be a *first mover*, you should consider being a *fast follower*. Fast followers can benefit a lot by the progress along the way paved by the first mover. However, becoming a fast follower also takes skills closely related to the skills associated to innovation culture. You need to develop the ability to scout and also the ability to adapt your organization to new possibilities. This takes curiosity, risk handling, ability to change, acceptance for failures, make future projections and so on. The step to go from a fast follower to a first mover might not be that large, and perhaps a fast follower could be a natural first step for *late followers* to progress. Because lagging behind over time as a late follower is not sustainable and might prove detrimental over time.

34 Get started – form a radical innovation group

Chapter summary

This chapter is about how to take the first step towards using future scenarios as guides to make the best strategic plans, plans that include elements of activities or products beyond the current and even plans that can outcompete the current. More specifically, the chapter is about how to initiate an effective radical innovation group, whose responsibility is to generate viable future concepts as potential building blocks for a total future scenario.

You will hear more about the following.

- Keep the group small – maximum six to seven people, and from there increase the number of groups instead of increasing the group size.
- The importance of having a fixed core group and invite competence beyond as required.
- The need to meet physically for innovation work, but how general information exchange can take place by remote conversations, like over phone or video communication.
- Virtual teams, which means borrowing people from around the company for regular short work sessions, without moving them organizationally.
- Which personal skills are important to be functional in a group like this:

  - Have an in-depth knowledge (expertise level) within a field
  - Additionally have a shallower understanding of as wide a field around the specific expertise level as possible
  - Be an optimistic and positive person
  - Individual creativity is an advantage but not as important as the collective creativity
  - Have the ability to visualize, mentally for oneself and paper/blackboard/screen to communicate clearly with others
  - Have good social skills
  - And much more

- The importance of the groups multiskill composition and why.
- The need for a facilitator.
- A systematic approach to innovation (both incremental and radical), which starts with a clear understanding of a customer need (More about on need-based innovation).

And finally, that this process generates radical innovation over and again through long-term systematic work and that you no longer need to rely on coincidences or ever worse, rely on magic to find real, new opportunities of a different nature.

Build a group and a meeting structure

If you have decided to be more systematic about also the radical part of innovation, the first thing you need to kick off is a way to systematically generate future possibilities or viable future scenarios. A great way to start is to generate a radical innovation group. The next chapter (*INTEGRATE – FIT INNOVATION GROUPS INTO YOUR ORGANIZATION*) will speak about how to scale up the effort when this group is efficient, so for now let us focus on this first single group.

However, before this I would like to ask you to do an experiment with me that may illustrate an essential feature about an important theory later in the book. Most of us have taken a plane, and many are even frequent flyers who have spent hours in airports and in planes time and time again waiting to get to your destination. I would like you right here and now to think about what you can imagine would be the next big thing in the aviation industry. Write it down somewhere where you can find it when this subject is brought back up again later in the book (in the chapter *IMPLEMENT – TAKE OUT THE FULL VALUE POTENTIAL*). Don't just skip this or leave a few open thoughts in your short-term memory. Take a few minutes and think about how airports and planes will develop time forward, make a few notes that we can revert to later and perhaps this can help you understand better basic theories presented in this book.

And now that the notes are made, let's continue to build a small efficient radical innovation muscle that can help the company stay in the forefront.

The main idea is to bring the right representatives from different parts of the company together to work in a systematic way on the company's challenges and yield valuable conceptual possibilities of a different nature tested beyond "showstoppers" on a regular basis. The group will function as a virtual team in the company, which in this context means a team forming for a limited time occasionally beyond the formal organizational structure.

Facilitator

First you need to appoint a facilitator. This person's main tasks will be to:

- find challenges to work on, and clearly frame the search to make sure everyone understands where innovation is wanted at each particular work session and where not to go (see *Shepherd leadership and framing the search* page 85)
- invite people to form an optimal group for the task at hand
- fix meeting formalities

    - set regular meeting time
    - reserve room or venue

- create a good atmosphere for innovative work by

    - build psychological safety (see *Relational skills and social intelligence* on page 54)
    - make sure everyone present participates actively during the meeting
    - challenge during the innovative process to assure sufficient stretch, but at the same time not go too far
    - keep up the good spirit (laughter and creativity have a close relation!)

        - take mental breaks when energy drops
        - preferably use humor actively (never too busy to share a good laugh)

- make sure progress stays within the frame of the search
- sum up results and facilitate the collective choice about which concept(s) to pursue further
- follow up tests between meetings and report results

- distribute funding and be responsible for the budget
- communicate concepts beyond the group to build confidence and active support
    - systematically build sustainable external confidence in the group, which is closely linked to success story telling

The facilitator needs to spend more time working with and for the group than the others, perhaps from 50% up to 100% of his/her time. The personality, skills or characteristics one should look for in the facilitator are the same as for the Core group members, see below under *Core group members* on page 46, but in addition he/she must have:

- knowledge of and passion for the innovation process
- a good network
    - particularly in the strategy department
    - knowing which channels are likely to support radical suggestions and
    - knowing which are likely to resist or sub optimize the content
- knowledge about the company's strategic direction
- knowledge of megatrends in society (which forms a basis for looking ahead)
- persistence (a lot of persistence)
- ability to hold convincing presentations

Facilitator tasks before the meeting

Preparations before the meeting are collected under the heading "administrative work" in Figure 7. These include defining the subject to work on and designing the optimal group to challenge the chosen subject.

The subject to work on can come from many places. What is important, though, is to make sure the chosen subject addresses a real business need in the company[10]. Later we will speak more specifically about the importance of need-based innovation to succeed with systematic radical innovation.

Receiving an order from an internal "innovation customer" is always best. First and foremost, it assures there is a real need supported by genuine desire. It normally also assures a formal anchor in the company when results start to come and extended funding is needed for testing. Another good source for challenges is a possible strategy document, which also assures a business need, although it may not come with a concrete innovation customer (the anchor). Other possibilities are always dilemmas or challenges group members see, but then a link to a real need in the company needs to be made. Addressing a clear business need will help implementation at a later stage.

Inviting the correct people can indeed be challenging, but the carrot is that half of the job is done when a great team is in place. Invitees can be chosen from three different groups in addition to the core group.

1. Problem owners or people knowledgeable on the problem at hand.
2. People with skills suited for radical innovation work and that fit the multiskill matrix (see *Core group members* on page 46 for more on multiskills).
3. Key personnel that can play an important role on a later stage to assure their early involvement and ownership.

For invitees in Categories 2 and 3 above, I would like to underline one useful consideration. If the facilitator can imagine some probable directions in which solutions can be found for a specific challenge, it may be advantageous to make sure there is knowledge in the group about these directions. For example, if you are working to improve the efficiency of a farm a hundred plus years ago in pre-tractor times and you are looking at alternatives to horses, as a facilitator you may suspect that the alternative solution may involve a new exciting product you have heard about called the combustion engine. Then it may be wise to make sure the group contains knowledge about combustion engines. This takes some creative thinking by the facilitator prior to the meeting. This is one of the reasons why those innovative skills are also important in the facilitator and not only the other group members.

One could argue that the facilitator in this way influences the result, a result that should be totally unbiased. I would say the positive sides of this outweigh the down sides. My experience is that if you tell innovative people that the solution can be found within one of two given directions, they will immediately start to challenge this claim and look for a third and even a fourth direction. Listing two directions will therefore quickly result in more than the two, if more than two exist. Not listing any by fear of planting any bias, will delay bringing everyone to the two directions, and even longer to the third and fourth.

Another task that can prove to be really useful, which also takes some imagination upfront, is arranging visual effects to be used during ideation work. This is about creating information points around which discussions can take place. These could be posters on the wall or physical models that could provide useful information, helping to spark new ideas. In our horse/tractor example, such posters could be drawings of a steam engine and/or a model of a locomotive in a train set (which was available before the tractor was invented). It could also be process diagram of the combustion cycle and/or a schematic overview over tasks normally performed on a farm. All of this could be useful information in the process of inventing the tractor and could be possible to think of before the innovative session after some considerations of which direction the innovative work could take. It is all about facilitating a good innovative session.

Facilitator tasks during the meeting

A particularly important skill necessary for the facilitator to master in action when facilitating radical innovation sessions is social intelligence. This is indeed an important skill for core members too, but even more so for the facilitator. This is first and foremost to make everyone feel at ease and from there to pull everyone actively into the discussion. In a multi skill group, this means in practical terms to bring all skills into the discussion. However, everyone active in the discussion is not enough. The facilitator needs to create the psychological safety needed for the contributors to mentally explore and openly share out-of-the-box ideas too, and this is the real challenging part for the facilitator. But there are several things the facilitator can do to enhance the psychological safety:

1. Humor is a key enabler (see *Humour* page 55). Humor makes shoulders come down and people open up. With humor and laughter it seems like those crazy contributions not leading to anything, those that we are so afraid to share, are considered a contribution to the fun part and somehow not a failure. As such, humor can be regarded as a safety net.
2. Bring the discussion from the present and into the future (see *Philosophy for creating radical ideas* page 62). This tends to disarm much of the resistance a proposal can meet with respect to practical problems. For example, if a candidate suggests a new concept in the present time, someone can argue that certain aspects of the idea are not possible due to rightful technological limitations or perhaps public regulations and the like. This can take the energy out of a direction that after a few iterations could have proven really valuable. If the same proposal was moved a number of years into the future, the proposer could defend him or herself by saying that this aspect will surely be solved by this point in time, allowing the exploration to continue with a noted soft spot.
3. The basic idea of using a Core Group who repeatedly show up to these creative sessions is to bring about psychological safety. When group members know each other well and have spent a lot of time exploring out-of-the-box ideas together, the necessary trust is built. Trust is the foundation for psychological safety. This will also positively influence guests too, as long as the guests do not outnumber the core team. Guests need particular attention to get quickly into a productive state of mind, and that is everyone's responsibility. After all, the effectiveness of any group is the collective creativity, where guests play an important part.
4. If a session is difficult to get out-of-the-box, so to say, the facilitator can set a precedence by proposing real out-of-the-box ideas him or herself. Offering a way may help even if the ideas themselves are useless. Since useless ideas are what everyone seems to be so afraid of, this effort may well get the ball rolling by taking some of the "heat" from the shoulders of others.

5. Influencing the way people talk to each other during the meeting is also linked to psychological safety. This is about talk in general, but particularly about feedback on proposals. A positive environment for co-creation focuses on ideas as building blocks whether they will become a part of the end solution or remain only an intermediate state. In this context, the briefest intermediate states are what certain other environments would refer to as a failed suggestion. *A building environment is an opposite of an elimination environment where there is a need to evaluate whether a suggestion is good or bad.* In a building environment there is no need to determine whether an idea is good or bad. The best ideas will survive as self-standing ideas or merge with others to create new possibilities, and those not needed will fade away in silence (we will elaborate further on this later in the book).
6. Another thing the facilitator can arrange for is food. Making social and relational progress over food is a tradition most places on our planet. Starting the meeting with free lunch brought to the meeting room can be a very efficient start of the meeting. The group starts with informal talk while eating and with time drifts into productive talk. This is indeed a nice reward for those giving some of their time to innovation and a brilliant way to build psychological safety from the beginning.

But the facilitator plays other important roles than creating psychological safety. A facilitator needs to make sure the group stays on track. In practical terms this means staying within the defined frames of the current innovation challenge (see *Shepherd leadership* on page 85). The group needs total freedom to explore within this framework, which is close to the core intention of an innovation group, but as soon as anyone drifts out of the frame of the day, the facilitator needs to remind this individual about the ongoing task and in this way guide him/her back on track. Targeted searches are a prerequisite for systemizing radical innovation[17].

An excellent way for the facilitator to kick off the innovative work on a newly given framework is to start exploring the frame with the group. I normally share some thoughts about different axes one can think along. These axes describe different fundamental directions on which a solution can be found, without stating anything about where on the axis the solution(s) might come. For example, if we are looking for new solutions to drive a car, an axis could be manual driving on the left, computer assisted manual driving in the middle and automatic driving to the right (see Figure 6 A). If we choose to look at future energy production, one axis could be large effective central energy producer with distribution system on one hand and local energy capture and use on the other (see Figure 6 B).

A)   Manual driving   Data assisted driving   Autonomous car

B)   Large central w/distribution   Distributed local capture and use

Figure 6   Example of axis to help analyze the search within the given innovation frame: A) the automation level of a vehicle and B) central vs. local energy production.

The axis can be backed up by fundamental questions that will inspire the group to think: How can we enhance the user experience? How can we fully automatize this process? How can we take advantage of the waste and turn it into a value? You may think now that sharing axes and questions may influence the group's free search and therefore impose a bias. As mentioned above, my experience is the opposite. If you tell innovative people that the solution can be found along two different axes, they would immediately challenge this statement and for example search for a third axis (see *Radical innovation not only for tomorrow but also today* on page 153).

Next to guarding the frame of the challenge and stimulate free thinking within the frame (e.g. proposing fundamental axes and asking basic questions), the facilitator needs to assure a sufficient stretch in the idea generation. The tendency is that people drift towards the familiar, which is the present solutions and the short time frame. A fundamental task of the facilitator is to assure the desired stretch in the idea generation towards the ultimate solution for the result to be valuable in a radical context (see *Philosophy for creating radical ideas* on page 62). Although the problem normally is *not to stretch far enough*, it is worth noting that assuring stretch also includes not *stretching too far*. For example, if you work with radical innovation on future transport, you may have gone too far if your ultimate solution is to send people from A to B atom-by-atom at the speed of light. Such a suggestion is probably too far into the future to inspire viable short-term solutions. Picking a specific year in the future to aim the innovation effort towards may guide the team to stretch appropriately in both directions.

The last facilitator task in the meeting is to round off the exploration work for the day, sum up what has been done and note which concepts the group members wish to pursue further. The group will also discuss how to advance the concept(s) chosen. This could be some sort of maturation or it could be handing it over to next stage (selling the concept internally). More than one innovative concept can be chosen. If there is disagreement, all innovative candidates with support are pursued and tests will guide which concept eventually will be the preferred.

Facilitator tasks after the meeting

After the meeting the facilitator's responsibility is to clean up the produced material which includes having hand sketches drawn up properly and clearly visualized and make the information ready for next stage. Relevant results need to be logged.

The next stage could be testing what the group proposed for further maturation (see next paragraph), in which case the facilitator organizes this testing. Or, the next stage could also be selling or handing over the product if the innovation team considers it finished and ready.

All of these tasks are collected under the heading "administrative work" in Figure 7.

Regular meetings

A really excellent way to structure the innovation work is to have regular innovation meetings, say 3 hours a week to mention a number, and work with practical and administrative matters like planning and preparing up-coming meetings, testing on-going concepts and selling mature concepts in between the meeting, like illustrated in Figure 7.

Figure 7 This circle illustrates a time cycle for the radical innovation group: A small part is regular Innovative meetings with the entire group and invited guests, while the rest of the time the facilitator does Administrative work like preparing meetings, working with ongoing concepts and promoting mature concepts.

Obviously, the meeting frequency doesn't have to be every week, and the duration can be longer and shorter than 3 hours. The important part is regularity. In addition, the ideation efficiency of such a group and the time administrative work takes between meetings, demands fairly short innovative sessions and much time between sessions.

All group members contribute during the innovative meetings, in the mentioned example those were 3 hours a week. Only the facilitator contributes beyond this. As an effect of the low contribution by the other participants beyond the dedicated innovation group meetings, they can remain organizationally attached to the department from which they came. This has several really positive effects on radical innovation efforts:

1   Each participant gets a mental refill in their normal roles in the company (as opposed to a person 100% recruited for radical innovation work). They will pick up challenges and solution principles they can bring to the table in the radical group work setting. Working regularly with challenges to find solutions will make people more alert to both challenges and potentially good solutions in the rest of their activities – a true innovation culture builder.
2   The radical innovation effort doesn't show up on any organizational map. This makes it more anonymous in the company, seen from both the inside and not least from the outside. Discreteness can in certain contexts be an advantage, like when working with controversial concepts for example with strong effect on manning, or to tone down radical efforts for investors. However, it is not particularly good for the innovation

culture building, which then is limited to what participants bring back to their organizational affiliation.
3   The group can be really dynamic, and changes can take place easily.
4   Each member can be inside champions for the different radical concepts in their respective organizational units, which is particularly important during the tough implementation phase. They will also be good innovation ambassadors for general innovation culture building.
5   And last but not least, the facilitator may choose group members amongst the very best candidates in the company (and beyond). Most people have the flexibility to set aside a few hours a week for work most often perceived as rewarding, knowledge building and energy providing. If the radical innovation work would require a significant portion of the candidate's position, the number and particularly the quality of the group candidates would reduce dramatically.

 Cutting a flower from its roots greatly effects its ability to continue blossoming.

Core group members

The facilitator builds up the core group by picking up three to five fellow colleagues from around the company or even beyond. It is absolutely crucial to build a multiskill team (see Figure 9), particularly when it comes to knowledge and expertise, but also other factors like gender, cultural background, company division/department and more (illustrated in Figure 8). There is obviously a limit for how many variations one can achieve in such a small group, but variation should be the core value in all but a couple of personal skills. Based on years of experience, I would say that the personality, skills or characteristics one should look for in all candidates, including the facilitator, are

- Optimism (to my opinion the most important one)
- Creativity (but not as important as one may think)

- Ability to visualize (both mentally for oneself and by drawings/sketches to others)
- Be an expert in something relevant (however within a field different from the other members)
- A wide know-how reaching far beyond the expert area (see Figure 11)
- Analytical skills and the ability to see core functions, key services and fundamental relations needed to solve the challenge
- Social intelligence
- Humor
- Curiosity

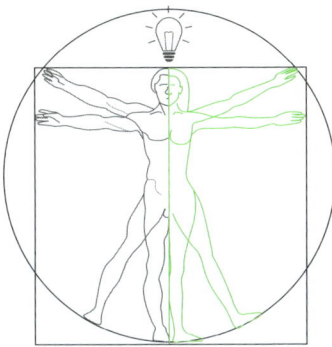

Figure 8 Many personal skills and characteristics are needed to function optimally as a core member in a radical innovation group. But even more important than individual characteristics are the collective diversity and the group mix of personal characteristics.

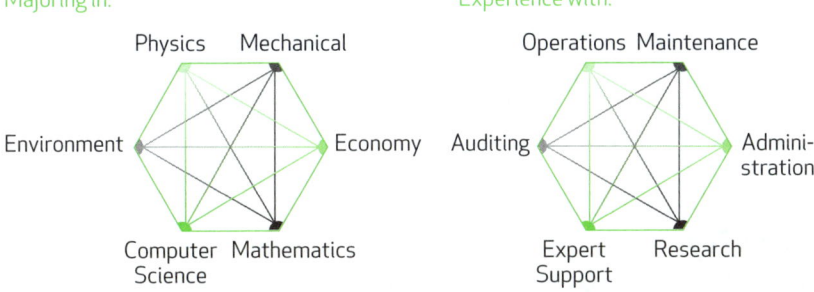

Figure 9 An example of how a multiskill group of six can look with respect to education and experience, and how they all interact. The example shows only two skills. Many other skills and personal characteristics are relevant in addition to these two.

Below is more about why the abovementioned personality, skills or personal characteristics are important for the different radical innovation group members.

Optimism

Looking at the number of ideas brought up in a radical innovation group compared to how many ideas actually get implemented, it is clear that the probability for success is very limited (if success can be limited to direct implementation only, which I would argue against). To continue making a serious effort to develop new solutions and really stretch imagination just a bit longer than what feels comfortable every time, takes an optimistic attitude almost to the limit of naivety. It is not hard to imagine that when a concept you have worked hard to build, made significant break-throughs on and that you are convinced will make a significant improvement are being heavily criticized and stopped, it takes an optimist to mobilize the same passion and energy behind the next challenge at hand. And the next again. Even more so when this happens time and time again. It is indeed important for a radical group to evaluate and somehow reward themselves (in addition to the more formal company reward system – see *INCENTIVES AND CULTURE – MAKE SUSTAINABLE GROWTH* on page 170). See also More about below.

This doesn't mean that less optimistic and even negative-oriented people are not needed in the radical innovation process. Negativity is a useful skill when a concept needs scrutiny. However, this skill must be used with care and social intelligence.

Creativity

One would expect that creativity is the most important personal skill in a radical innovation group, and this is partly true, but just partly. The most important skill is the collective group creativity, and this is far from the sum of each group member's individual creativity. It is more a sum of all relevant personal skills of all group members, how all these skills interact and how they play well with each other, which is why it could be useful also to look beyond the creativity side when considering a potential group candidate. However, creativity is indeed one of the personal skills important for a radical innovation group. Other important and closely related skills are the ability to share creative contributions, allow others to change parts of the contribution and even put the contribution fully aside for better ideas. Likewise, the ability to contribute constructively when someone else has a suggestion and genuinely work hard to improve that foundation is important for the group effectiveness. This brings us slowly over to another important skill for a radical innovation group; social skills (see below). But before we leave creativity, I would like to add that creativity could be well hidden, and I would claim creativity is wider spread than our eyes can see. A well-functioning group will bring out creativity in guests who did not know of its presence in themselves. All these sides of creativity are reasons why I recommend to tone the creativity skill down and certain other skills, like optimism, up when considering a new member for a radical innovation group.

More about...

...how an idea could advance and why optimism is a key personal quality for a member of a radical innovation group.

Optimism is really one of the key personal qualities for members in a radical innovation group. One reason is linked to the iterative progress in the concept development combined with the most frequent end result – termination.

Let us look at an example of how an imaginary concept development can proceed (see figure 10 on page 50). In this illustration the x-axis refers to the number of users benefiting from the invention while the y-axis is a measure of how radical the solution is. The green line represents the progress of the imaginary concept from its start in Point 1, which is the present solution. In an innovative process it may be beneficial to work with a concrete case. After one innovation cycle (one pass in Figure 13), the first solutions may therefore be beneficial for this particular case (green Point 2). It may not be beneficial for other similar users that were not taken into account in our work with a specific case. Eric Ries' Lean Startup[2] tells us that we should go out and get feedback on our progress, and make adjustments if necessary. The positive feedback in this case will at best be limited to our special case and no one else.

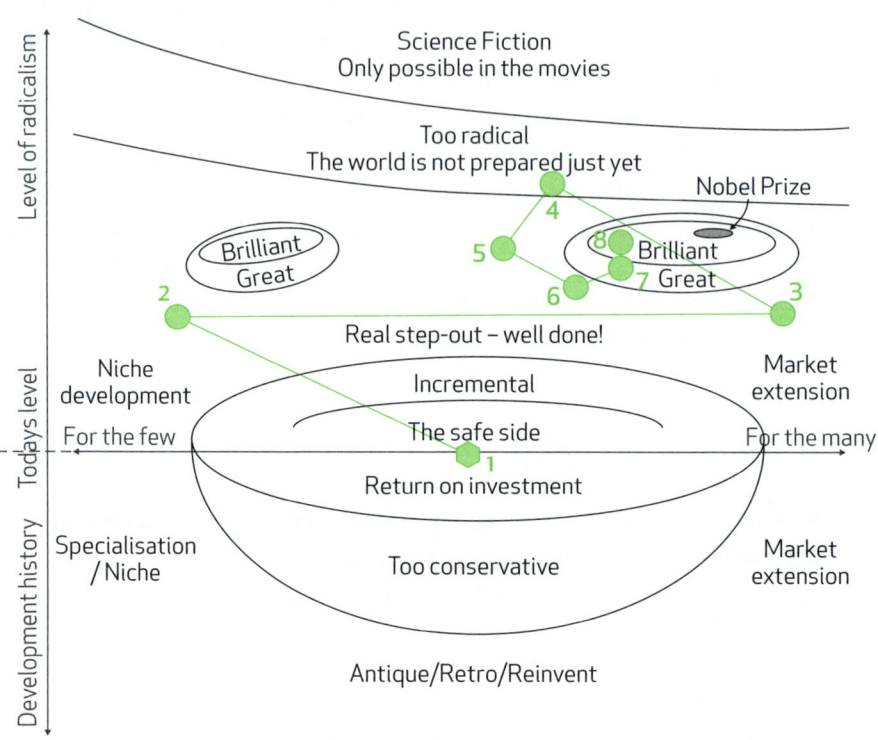

Figure 10 Description of how a new concept can advance through numerous iterations drawn as a green graph where the x-axis (grey) is a measure of the applicability and the y-axis (also grey) is a measure of how radical the concept is. The red lines divide the area into parts and the associated text describes characteristics with each area.

As a result, we may apply the 10X technique (do the second loop of Figure 13) to increase the applicability of our concept. This will take us from Point 2 over to 3, on the right side of the graph. Our concept is now beneficial for a wide range of users, and as such a more fundamentally solid solution. The feedback is now good from a wide range of users, but we can still not build enthusiasm for our concept. This is probably because the concept is not that different to what is known today, not enough for anyone to take the additional risk normally associated with a new direction as an alternative to the comfortable, known one.

We may therefore try to adjust more in the radical direction, Point 4, just to find out that we went too far. We have now good feedback and can sense enthusiasm, but nobody dares moving forward to this risky endeavor. We make a new innovation loop like described in Figure 13, and manage to improve the concept's attractiveness by making it less radical (Point 5). Now we get customers interested, and one is even willing to co-fund. At this point we would have chosen to freeze the concept and move to the next development stage, but we meet a challenge with a sub-solution we thought would be straightforward and it wasn't. We involve the paying customer and continue to explore in our strive for excellence. As we iteratively work our way via great (Point 7) to brilliant (Point 8) we decide our solution is more than good enough, we freeze the overall concept, and move to next development stage, not realizing that we are seriously close to something that could change history and qualify for a Nobel Prize.

From imaginary example and back to why optimism is so crucial for radical innovation. To keep on working energetically on the mission through disappointment after disappointment with feedback all the way from balanced to irrational, and not only stay motivated but even sharpen the efforts by raising assignment complexity, takes special skills. Furthermore, in the example above the concept was accepted, funded and taken further. This is actually exceptional. Most radical efforts lead to nothing, no matter the quality of the group. In fact, if a group has a high success factor, they haven't stretched far enough. They haven't used their full potential and should start to address more basic challenges with associated larger solutions with higher impact potential. This inherent uphill struggle meeting a constant headwind does indeed take special personal skills in which optimism can be found at the very core.

Visual

The ability to visualize is very important for members in a radical innovation group for several reasons. First and foremost, it is about sharing thoughts, which after all is core for productivity. In a truly multiskill group, there is no such thing as common terminology and only low-level shared knowledge platforms. In order to share thoughts quickly and efficiently, visual illustrations are really important. They bring the group together conceptually, mentally and even physically around the drawing. They have the ability to bring others "into your thoughts" in a moment, and with a good illustration, the visitor will have a tendency to stay there as well. Human beings have based their impressions on images for millions of years, while the written words have only been around for a thousand years or so. Most illustrations are much easier to remember than written or spoken words between work sessions, which is when a lot of maturation is done. These illustrations can be simple sketches during a work session, but it can be advantageous to draw them more thoroughly between sessions. I would recommend not to outsource turning sketches into proper drawings out of the innovation group. A lot of dilemmas and possibilities come up when things get more concretized through a re-drawing process.

However, there are more reasons for being visual. Radical innovation is about envisioning the future. Before a thought can be shared in a group, it needs to enter a mind. I would claim that the ability to visualize not only a future situation (like an image), but also building, comparing and testing different scenarios mentally (more like a video in the head) is a great advantage for someone who would like to predict the future. To the extent that this envisioning can be composed of contributions from more than one individual and exist in more than one head, you have the full visual capacity sought by a radical innovation group.

Mental visualization can with advantage be assisted by relevant posters and models available in the room where the creative process takes place. These can unite the group in discussions, help the mental work and spark new ideas, all of which is excellent for creative sessions.

And finally, being visual is also important when selling a concept to an Idea Receiver (someone who can assist in developing and commercializing the concept inside or outside the company; see *INCENTIVES AND CULTURE – MAKE SUSTAINABLE GROWTH* on page 170. The reasons this is important are the same as for sharing your thoughts within the group – effective communication of potentially complex matters.

Deep and wide knowledge

Knowledge is an important asset for any innovation group. Together with the multiskill requirement, a radical innovation group should have in-depth knowledge within several disciplines, all of which can and will be useful while working. However, to awaken the collective creativity it is important that the different centers of expertise somehow meet to create common ground, so to say. It is therefore key for members to have a breadth of let's say more shallow knowledge around their point of expertise. The wider this knowledge is, the better because where this knowledge and experience overlap between group members, innovation gold can be found, or innovation seeds can be sown (see Figure 11).

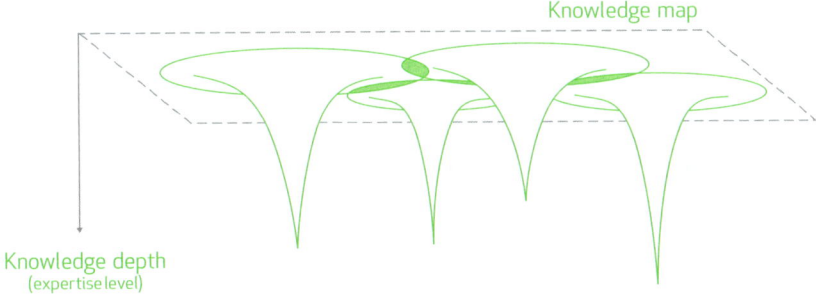

Figure 11 Illustration of how expertise levels should be distributed in a radical innovation group and how the breadth of their knowledge and experience should overlap. In the overlaps (green in the figure) innovation gold can be found.

Relational skills and social intelligence

A virtual team is not the same as organizational affiliation. Many people could feel uncomfortable in virtual teams for different reasons. Things like distance to close colleagues and line manager, breaking daily routines, challenging own competence, and even weaker links to appraisal and performance score could be some of the reasons why many would hesitate to join a radical group for a few hours a week.

Once in the virtual team, the work can also be perceived as socially challenging. When somebody comes forward and propose a new ground-breaking idea, they put themselves in a somewhat delicate position. Metaphorically it can be somewhat similar to getting naked in public, since many feel they expose themselves to an extent when suggesting things they are really unsure about and/or they think is new to the world. To prepare the ground for a flow of these situations, relational skills and social intelligence are very important in building a culture of psychological safety.

These are the main reasons why a fixed core group is necessary. The core group will be familiar with each other, know each other's strengths, weaknesses, abilities and limitations. This reduces the barrier against both participating and proposing "out of the box" suggestions. It increases the tolerance for receiving feedback on the proposals as well. All of this is lubricated by relational skills and social intelligence amongst the participants, which ideally should be two of the most important criteria for a potential member's candidacy in the group. Building up a mutual trust and respect are very important for the core group to be efficient in the sense that no idea or proposal is too scary to bring forward. Assuring and building this psychological safety is one of the facilitator's most important tasks, although it is the responsibility of every member.

Sharing a wild idea can feel like getting naked in public.

In a psychological safety context, another important side of a well-functioning core group is how it will positively influence invited guests. Even reserved and careful guests are likely to catch up quickly and join the creative process if the core group shows open and fearless idea exploration without hesitating to get "creatively naked" and simultaneously shows generosity to the "failing" attempts. The core group will take the lead and gradually disarm the guest's fear of these types of awkward situations as long as the number of guests does not outnumber the core group. Large groups are not efficient anyway. It is all about bringing everyone in the room into a relaxed, open and creative state of mind.

Humor

After years of experience facilitating radical innovation groups and other innovative settings, I have become convinced that there is a direct relationship between laughter and being innovatively productive. The more creative we are, the more we laugh and have fun. I am not sure it is equally true the other way around. You can definitely be in an enjoyable mood without necessarily being creative. But I am sure that when you do have fun laughing, you are in a better position to be creative than if you were in a less enjoyable mood. Connections between fun and creativity can possibly be found on different levels down to the release of hormones stimulating the brain to be creative, but this is just a guess. What can be observed in an innovation context, though, is that laughter seemingly is a way to relax and to stop worrying about saying stupid things. Stupid things will be considered a "fun-fact" and therefore a contribution to the ambience, which is a comfortable psychological safety net if a suggestion does not reach the selected few and taken on further. This has a really positive effect on creativity and can be taken advantage of in creative sessions by facilitating a good ambience. This is of course also linked to the social skills of all participants including the facilitator.

 Laughter and creativity have a mutual dependency.

Curiosity

Curiosity is the last of the personality skills and characteristics listed in this section, but it is certainly not the least important. The sum of all the individuals' curiosity adds up to the collective group curiosity, which fuels the whole innovation process. It is in the core of what drives the group forward, just next to optimism, both of which make up an explosive combination. Perhaps this effect is best seen in small children. Faced with significant problems like "peace on earth", they tend to talk while breathing both in and out, and listing one great suggestion after the other, wondering what the effect of each one would be.

Curiosity and disagreements or let's say, friction, make up a really interesting combination. In other contexts, friction between individuals is regarded as negative. In an innovation setting, friction met with curiosity and optimism can lead to great possibilities and is a positive asset more than a treat. Also, friction between an individual and the company's prevailing system, process, product or practice is in the same manner a seed for great changes if it is diminished by optimistic curiosity. Curiosity is a great individual characteristic for a person in a radical innovation group.

More about...

...NEED-BASED INNOVATION and why targeted innovation starts with a need.

There are principally two different ways to merge a customer need with a new solution:

1. You could search for great solutions, and twist and tweak them to see if they somehow can meet the needs we find customers have, or we could even create new needs. An example of the latter is that not many people knew they needed a tablet like the iPad before it was introduced. A need was created and this need is now well established.

2   You can start by understanding a customer need and try to develop a solution to that particular need.

Both ways work and there are many examples throughout history in each category. However, Category 1 in my opinion has more coincidence associated to progress then Category 2. You can argue that Category 1 is about searching for *something* for *someone*, which is not a particularly targeted approach. This may work well for an independent freelance or for start-up companies that have few established assets. These groups can get ideas more coincidently over time perhaps in different contexts, and decide that one of 1000 ideas is good enough to be pursued. When the ideas turn into nice solutions which seemingly fill a customer (future?) need, they can ramp up to create value. Ramp up in this context could include building a thorough understanding of the need potential (test a minimum viable product), get competence to develop a product (or service), build production capacity, a marketing strategy in a new field and set up a sales structure in this new segment. Basically, it seems to me Category 1 fits those who can spend recourses on an untargeted search over time and have the flexibility to adapt to anything when a possibility arises.

For established companies, Category 1 is challenging. A totally free search is not in alignment with an overall strategic direction (unless the strategy is "go anywhere"). They also lack the necessary organizational flexibility to adapt to whatever comes out of the search. Established companies need to get the most out of their knowledge base, experience and their physical assets like production facilities, marketing and sales structure. This is all about strategic direction and gathering together to move in this direction. In this perspective Category 2 (see bullet list above) is more suitable for established companies of a certain size. To start with a need makes the whole process more systematic and targeted, which is almost a requirement to create a systematic and predictable process. "Systematic and predictable" in this context means to be able to apply a specific approach with a given resource base and expect an even flow of high-quality results. This becomes more and more challenging the more the process steps are left to coincidence.

A main objective with this book is to also offer a method to *systemize* radical innovation. Therefore, I would strongly recommend starting the innovation process with a clear understanding of the customer need that we would like to radically change. This is often referred to as *need-based innovation*[10], which is about finding out what the customer needs and trying to find solutions for these needs. Some use the term "search for meaning" instead of "finding customer needs". These two are quite close but not exactly the same. Perhaps meaning asks you to search more within yourself, while need is more linked to studying the customer. Either way, need or meaning make up a base for framing the search, the importance of which will be explained later in the book (see *Shepherd leadership* on page 85), where the need concept also is explained more in detail. The need will remain a mental anchor throughout the process, which guides all the participants. In a later chapter (see *Radical innovation not only for tomorrow but also today* page 153) we will also see how we can take advantage of mental anchors by replacing the current need with a radical future scenario (which in this context can be seen as a future need) in order to motivate further broadening of the ongoing incremental innovation efforts. This is probably where the real value can be found in radical innovation for medium-to-large companies.

 Targeted innovation starts with the business need.

Implement efficient innovation work methods that yield radical results

One of the keys to radical innovation success, particularly in a company that normally works in incremental innovation mode, is to apply a work method that yields radical innovation and not incremental.

In this section we will look at:

- some fundamental differences between work methods that result in incremental solutions on one hand and radical solutions on the other
- propose a philosophy that takes the focus away from the present solution and into the future
- detail a work method for the radical innovation group built on this philosophy.

In the context of work methods, it might also be of interest to look through *Appendix A: Academic perspective by Dr. Ingunn Johanne Ness* on page 196. Here the brilliant senior researcher, Dr. Ingunn Johanne Ness, who followed our group closely over almost two years, shares some of her insights and findings from an external perspective while studying our radical innovation pilot group.

Work methods associated with incremental innovation

Most improvement projects start with an analysis of the current situation. Let us say that we are after a cost reduction of something. The likelihood is that we analyze the cost structure to find out where the largest potential for cost savings are, and then we plan how to improve these areas to achieve our cost saving potential. Analyses can be followed by a Continuous Improvement method to systematically meet the saving potential step-by-step. As another example, let us say we want to improve the dimensional tolerances on a set of mechanical parts in a gear box that eventually will be mounted together and make up a total error. We start by analyzing all tolerances. Continuous Improvement suggests that you measure all relevant tolerances, order them from the highest contributor to the smallest, and initiate projects on the largest contributors with the highest impact on the overall precision. Given that the project is successful, another parameter will be the largest next time you measure – now you start working on the largest contributor at this point. These types of analyses of the current situation are a highway to incremental improvements, which, by all means are very important, but not the only way to improve. What is common to projects starting with an analytical approach of the current solution is that the known solution remains in the center of attention all the time. You even *zoom into* the current solution to find the "guilty" part. Furthermore, analysis in this context means dividing the solution into segments to be measured. This focuses your attention on each individual segment without questioning improvement potentials of the totality. Then the new solution is very likely to contain all segments of the current solution and as such come out near the current solution too. As a result, you have to justify how to change the current solution. This can be referred to as the *Justify out method* and is well adapted for incremental innovation (see summary in Figure 27).

Horse example

Now, if we jump back 100 to 150 years and we find ourselves on a farm, which in those days was really dependent on their hard working horses, let us imagine that we want to improve the overall performance of the farm, which at the time was closely linked to the performance of the farm's horses. Then we could (and should) bring in horse experts. They would spend lots of time to analyze the current situation and would surely come up with a long list of improvement suggestions – those would quite likely be of incremental nature in the sense that they would be about horses and how their performance can be improved (better food mix, improved work and rest procedures, upgraded stable conditions etc.). But would they come up with the tractor as an improvement proposal (before the tractor existed)? This would be doubtful. And the day the tractor concept was born on this planet, would you consider it likely that it was built on a detailed analysis of the horses' performance from all possible view angles? I would say no. Chopping the horse's performance into segments doesn't answer your question about whether or not the horse is the right solution. Performance drop is another issue. It probably took the tractor many years to outperform the horse on most of the tasks for which the horses held responsibility. So, if a comparative performance analysis was made between horse and tractor in that "project", the new solution would come out negative to the advantage of the horse and would probably have been discarded.

I don't know the details about the invention of the tractor, but based on the experience of giving birth to numerous other radical concepts, I would consider it likely that the following list separated the situation at the birth of the tractor to a more normal group of horse experts giving the farmer advice on how to get more out of his/her horses.

- the focus was not on the present solution (horses)
- the expertise present stretched way beyond horses and included knowledge bases like other vehicles, machines and combustion, general farming, advancement in rough terrain by wheels etc. (maybe all within the same person)
- there was an understanding of the fundamental functions of horses in farming (like providing consistently reliable power everywhere) and no focus on details
- when analyzing the challenge they did not *zoom in* to find which part of the horse had the largest improvement potential, but, on the contrary *zoomed out* to build an understanding of the more fundamental challenges or dilemmas associated with use of horses in farming (I guess things like sickness, temperature dependency, power limitations, moods, heavy "maintenance", food/drink demand, rest requirements etc.), again without focus on details
- the ability to think far ahead – imagining a machine that could take over all the tasks of the horse and multiply the provided power without pauses of any sort (although it took many generations of tractors before the world saw anything near that performance)
- and finally I would not be surprised if the inventor(s) applied the *justify in method* when creating the tractor – which in this case means that he/

she/they started with nothing and added things necessary to meet the fundamental needs (such as: "I need more than ten times the power of a horse – I need an engine and a power outlet. How to bring the engine around in nature? I need wheels on the engine – oh, perhaps I can use some of the power via the wheels or belts to bring the construction around in nature…").

Philosophy for creating radical ideas

The horse example above is meant to illustrate what is needed to make sure you aim for radical ideas, and at the same time demonstrate how this fundamentally is separated from incremental work.

To promote radical innovation, I would strongly recommend applying the following philosophy: *When faced with the initial perceived need, zoom out and find the fundamental underlying need or question to ask. Then look far into the future and start to build the* ultimate solution *from a blank sheet (see summary in Figure 27 on page 128).*

We will see later how we can materialize future solutions in a shorter time frame (see IMPLEMENT – TAKE OUT THE FULL VALUE POTENTIAL on page 148). But first some comments on the above statement. It all starts with a clear understanding of the real underlying need, found by asking the right questions that eventually will lead to a real solution (tractor example: how to get power consistently anywhere in nature). More dangerous than having wrong answers is the right answer to the wrong question[17]. The level at which you search for the need is also vital. If you want a radically new solution you cannot dive into the existing solution and feel "at home". For example, when starting your improvement work by dividing the current solution into groups and subgroups to measure and compare the parameter you are working on (like cost in a cost saving project), you have automatically accepted the main structure of the current solution. This technique is essential in incremental improvement systems like LEAN and Continuous Improvement, but it is a serious mistake if you want solutions of a different nature. Instead, you should zoom out, get an overview, seek the core need[10], the mother of all challenges in the current context, perhaps formulated as a "how to…" question, and keep this as a guiding star when you move far into the future and search for the ultimate solution.

If you don't know your way in the woods, don't bend down and study the soil under your shoes – climb the tallest tree.

"Far into the future" will vary quite a lot from challenge to challenge, and also vary on a higher level between different industries. While two years is a long time in the mobile phone industry, ten years is a short time in the heavy industry sector, for example metal sheet rolling. The main intention with looking far ahead is twofold. On one hand, you force yourself to concretize the end goal. This allows you to set the right direction. And when both the end goal and the direction is clear, it should be easier to decide on the best first step. Even if several options seem reasonable as a first step by an initial look, having the end goal in mind up front can help you make the best choice. This first step will obviously be more moderate than the ultimate solution, but it may be the first development of a new «S» curve (see the second curve in Figure 5b on page 25). The second objective in looking far ahead is to free the creative minds from present commonly known obstacles in the search for the ultimate. You are, for example, more likely to worry less about current rules and regulations, or specific technical challenges in the far future than developing next solution. You are more likely to say that cars are self-driving in ten years than the next model. This frees up creative potential.

When you are in the far future, exploring different ultimate situations can be quite enlightening. Different ultimate situations in this context means imagining extremities. As an example, let's say that we are working on the future of vehicles. Then we could ask ourselves, how would a vehicle for single people look and how would they look if they are made to transport a thousand people? How would a vehicle without wheels work, and how would you accomplish transport without a combustion engine, or rather, since we already have electric cars that meet this objective, let's say without any engine? Can we envisage a car as an integral part of other important useful objects and functions, like our living room (entertainment), our office (work) or even our bed (relaxation)? Or quite oppositely, can we disintegrate all the functions of a car totally (and get something even simpler than a Segway)? All of those silly vehicle situations can trigger something useful about future cars that we don't know of yet.

Building a new concept from nothing can be referred to as *justify in*, as opposed to *justify out*. When applying justify in, you have to argue adding something to your new concept, or said in a different way, you have to *justify* why you add something *in*to your new solution. This is yet another method to free yourself from the present solution. Let's say for simplicity that the present solution is built up as a binary tree of two decisions per level over five levels (see Figure 12). Using justify out will bring you back down the same branch towards the trunk. Applying justify in takes you from the root and into any direction. You are forced to reconsider every option and the outcome can be the entire tree. Justify in opens the solution space dramatically.

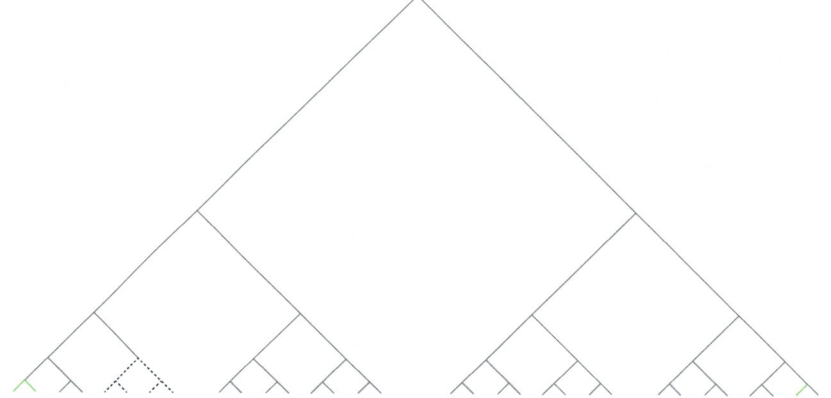

Figure 12 A binary tree of five levels illustrating the solution space of a solution with five levels of detail with only two options per level (which is a really simplified representation for illustrative purposes only). Justify out applied on one level gives the change illustrated in green, while justify out on two levels can give an impact extension shown in shown as dashed lines. Justify in would start at the root and could end up anywhere in the tree.

Let's look at an example. One of the large car manufacturers would like to increase their market share in the small city car segment, and analyses tell them that sales price is the main driver for sales. In a justify out scenario they would analyze their vehicle and perhaps they would find that the engine is the highest cost. Now they jump back one step in the binary tree above and re-evaluate the engine. In this attempt to cut engine cost they would end up in a discussion about pollution and environment, acceptable acceleration, consumption, weight/volume, maintenance friendliness, life expectancy and so on. The end result would be a compromise between all of the above and the cost reduction would be modest. In a justify in scenario, one would put the entire car aside and start to talk about what the customer fundamentally needs – which is exploring the root of the binary tree. A result of this exercise could be an electric bike with a nice grocery basket, which is an explosive market just now. This product has nothing in common with a traditional small combustion city car – it would be a radical solution.

Looking far into the future (see Figure 33 A) and applying justify in is a very powerful combination to achieve radical innovation. I would argue that it is more powerful than evolution, because it allows us to see the benefits in the future, which makes it more acceptable to have an intermediate dip in performance, something evolution cannot (see More about on 23). Like evolution, incremental innovation is dependent on progress for every increment.

At this point, it can be useful to briefly reflect upon why jumping far into the future is so easy to say but so very hard to do, particularly for larger organizations. To me this brings us straight into one of the factors that separates good leaders from the brilliant ones. Organizations appreciate management and leadership with a nose for those projects that deliver. A key promotion criterion is the ability to see those valuable projects through. The candidate must not only be able to separate poor projects from good, but also in a pool of good projects, good leadership picks the most promising and valuable, and eventually follows them all the way to value creation. Then the focus is on practical feasibility, risk management and delivery. In an organization full of stakeholders who have taken this art to the extreme over large parts of their careers, it can be quite challenging to propose as a first move in a new important project to go way into the future and explore ultimate solutions, which obviously appears far from feasible and you have to search for possibilities in an ocean of risk – unless the leader is of the brilliant type. Because the brilliant type of leadership will be able to *both* apply the feasibility, risk and delivery consideration on the incremental portfolio *and*, at the same time, comfortably explore the ultimate domain when radical solutions are sought. This is called ambidexterity [5-9] (ambidextrous leadership) – an ability that takes real leadership skills but can be very valuable when mastered well.

Work method for radical innovation

The horse example above illustrates much of the work process that would yield radical concepts rather than getting caught in the small steps of incremental innovation.

In addition to the multiskill team we spoke about in section *Build a group and a meeting structure* on page 36 (which strictly speaking is not a work method but a structural element) the following work steps are recommended.

1. Start with a challenge: Ask higher level questions to build a thorough understanding of the need (business or customer need). Use the need to clearly frame the search.
2. Premature ideation (optional): Spend a short time finding solutions before you are introduced properly to the problem.

    a. After the next bullet point you will no longer have the luxury to be totally uncolored by the existing solution. The current step will most of the time not give a lot, but the way you think here might prove to be valuable later.

3. Understand the task by zooming out: Spend a short time with the current solution in order to "peel the onion" and find the core challenge. At this point you want to work on finding the right question to ask, and later to solve. A good need statement can (Point 1 above) can be a good core challenge statement. Try to get information straight from the source,

live from people directly involved with the present solution and the challenges associated to the solution. Let us call them problem owners.

- a Establish the fundamental functions and services the solution needs to fulfil.
- b Spend time to understand fundamental challenges, dilemmas and connections
- c In a good session interviewing the problem owner and sharing insight into the challenge will slowly lead to the fundamental question that needs answering, which again gradually will turn into solution suggestions (this means that ideation is gradually starting already here).

4 Go extreme: look for the ultimate solution in a long-term perspective (but not too long).

- a Start with a blank sheet and add features needed to fulfil the basic functions (*justify in* method). Keep things as simple as possible.
- b Verify that the solution meets fundamental challenges and dilemmas.
- c Look for synergies and integration possibilities between sub-solutions and try to simplify further.
- d Visualize the solution as you build.
- e Do not worry about technical or business model gaps at this point, but build a complete concept down to a certain detail level.
- f Keep relevant megatrends in mind as a basis for a possible direction.

5 Step back from the future (if a shorter-term solution is required).

- a When the ultimate solution in the future is clear, start to look for how this solution could look in the time perspective for which you are aiming. Another way is to start working on a plan to get from the present to the ultimate solution, which obviously will take you through the desired level in a shorter time perspective while respecting the longer-term direction.

6   Upscale (the 10X method[28]): verify how the solution would look if you expand the intended customer segment and upscale the value proposal and applicability (zoom further out).
7   Rework or test: Go to Step 1 to see if the solution sufficiently meets the need or has to be further improved.

   a   Further improve: new cycle from Step 1 through 7.
   b   Sufficiently meeting the need: go to "proof-of-concept-testing". The aim here is, in a simple, quick and cheap way, to make sure the concept will work and that there are no showstoppers associated to the proposals.

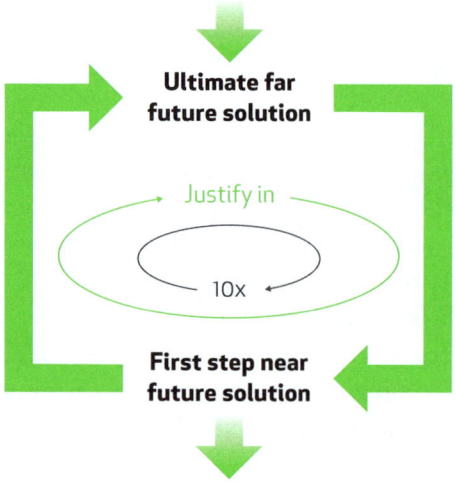

Figure 13   The work process to achieve radical results: You start by going for the Utimate solution in the far future by applying the Justify In method. When you have a solution you perform a 10X check. Now you take your solution back to the near future and see how it can be applied soon, still using justify in and 10X. When you learn new things, go back and update the Ultimate far future solution before yet again returning to the near present.

It is worth noting that Point 3, Understanding The Task, is about finding the fundamental function or service that we are trying to improve and converting this into the main question that needs answering. It is about taking the initially stated need and finding a higher version of it, a more general fundamental need closer to the root need. In the tractor example above, the question would typically not be "how can we get more power per hour out of each horse?". It would rather be "how to get power consistently anywhere in nature?" despite the customer saying, "I want a stronger horse". You can say that it is applying the 10X method on needs (for more on the 10X method, see comments below on Point 6). Within incremental innovation it is the opposite. Through analyzing the current solution you search for the specific problem(s), making the need as low level as possible, down to a concrete nut and bolt if necessary.

Let's look at an example of the above: we are a car manufacturer and we want to increase the margins on our next car model. In a *justify out* context we would log the cost of components and sub-components. We would also study the cost saving potential and what effect this would have on the quality. Based on this we would argue which components to change, while the overall change would stay very limited. The *justify in* method changes this limitation and forces you to rebuild the product and as such challenges its present design. Understanding the task by finding the fundamental need in the car example could typically be "get five persons from A to B". We would disregard all extras like "entertain five persons" (with reference to the stereo) or "keep five people cool on a warm day" (with reference to the air conditioning system). These may be added later if it fits the concept, but we are looking for the basic function here – to transport people. With this need in mind, we would start to build a new transportation device on white sheets. In a *justify in* context, the outcome is totally open while the *justify out* context keeps you locked within the old solution.

Before the list above we looked at the importance of Point 4, to Go Extreme. Going extreme before following Point 5, Step Back From The Future, has also an importance in achieving sustainable radical innovation. Without going extreme and way into the future several first steps can appear viable and some even better than what follows a future perspective. For example, when buying a new car, you can choose a petrol, a diesel or an electric option. If at present there are few charging stations and your home has only standard electric circuit in the vicinity of your parking, you may choose one of the two other options. However, if a future look may reveal that CO_2 taxes on fuel will rocket and number of charging stations explode, the choice of car may be different. Long-term perspectives may change how we look at today's options.

There is also another good reason for passing by the Ultimate solution before stepping back. In an improvement or development context looking far ahead first allows you to have the potential future solution in mind when designing the first step. A mental anchor on a future solution motivates the first step to be longer. This will be more thoroughly discussed in *IMPLEMENT – TAKE OUT THE FULL VALUE POTENTIAL* on page 148.

Incremental innovation potential is best assessed by experts.
Radical innovation potential
is best assessed by visionaries.

The Upscaling Point 6, the 10X method, also deserves a further comment. The upscaling exercise is about studying how the solution changes as the solution is adapted to new levels of customers. For example, if you are inventing a more practical car for the disabled in wheelchairs, upscaling could mean to check if your great new concept could function for other disabilities. You could continue to further upscale the concept for cars utilized also by the non-disabled, then for any kind of vehicle, and so on. During these exercises you may pick up valuable learning for every time the solution is scaled up, and the chance is that the potential impact/value can increase while your solution approaches a more fundamentally viable improvement. Intrinsically, this also means that the first case you work on when stretching your imagination going ultimate (Point 4) will not define the level of your final solution. In practical terms, you can start by working on a concrete and clear task, like the car for the disabled, and be well aware that you may still influence all vehicles (and beyond) through the 10X approach. Staring off exploring the ultimate solution with a clear and concrete case makes progress easier and motivation higher. And after all, if 10X doesn't bring you anywhere, I am sure our disabled friends will appreciate progress as you move on to the next project.

How to enter the room of opportunity

Over a period of about two years my radical group was observed by a Ph.D. student, Ingunn Johanne Ness, from the Faculty of Psychology at University of Bergen. She wrote her doctoral thesis[20] on creative processes in innovation groups and a significant part of her data came from her observations in our group. In this paragraph I would like to share some of her findings, as I believe they could be useful guidelines for anyone who like to systematically approach radical innovation.

Typical innovation sessions consisted of one diverging part where knowledge and creative opportunities was shared, and a converging part where a higher number of options were prioritized into a few and often just one. The diverging part started with the facilitator sharing a challenge rooted in a company business need. The challenge could also be proposed by one of the attendees. After the challenge was understood, the group entered into a knowledge sharing phase in order to build the collective knowledge in the group. This part normally started by the one who presumably knew most about the task at hand, which often was someone invited for that purpose. A typical observation Ingunn made was the smooth transition from knowledge sharing to creative phase, which she called *the room of opportunity*. In practical terms the group started by listening to the one sharing knowledge. Quite quickly technical questions started to arise accompanied by additional shorter knowledge contributions to the topic. Slowly the technical questions would turn into suggestions with questions starting with "Have you ever tried to…" and "why don't you try to…" In practical terms this was the slow beginning of the creative phase or the room of opportunity. Slowly these questions would turn into more comprehensive suggestions, which other member would start to build upon, and all of a sudden creativity was the majority of the conversation and the interval of time would increase between technical questions about the present solution. Along with the rise of the creative phase came the rise of the energy level and more group members would rise up from a more relaxed position to actively participate near the drawing board on the wall. During the best sessions, people could not wait for their turn to talk, and several people would talk simultaneously while drawings were updated several places at the same time.

In this phase ideas are produced, some bouncing from one person to the other while growing and changing. Some ideas obviously didn't grow in this phase, but disappeared irrevocably into the darker side of the collective memory. But little attention was given to these ideas and as such, no ideas, or at least very few, are explicitly rejected during this type of sessions. They simply didn't survive the room of opportunity at the expense of presumably better opportunities.

Towards the end of a session, the facilitator would step up and switch the meeting over from diverging creativity to converging prioritization. In practical terms, this would be the facilitator asking all the participants which idea to follow up further, and what would the participants like followed up in order to reduce uncertainty. It is worth noting that also at this point ideas would not explicitly be rejected, although many ideas would be left behind at the expense of those brought forward through the prioritization discussion. The follow up could be one favorite idea or a few choices. For more on Ingunn's work, see her summary of her contributions in Appendix A on page 196.

More about...

...the work method and how it could have been used to invent the tractor.
Let us imagine that a farmer in Texas, USA, in pre-tractor times wanted to improve his/her ability to plow the ground on his/her fields. He had clever friends in many fields and invited a real multiskilled team to work on the task.

1   Understand the task
Fundamental need: More reliable and consistent plowing around the soil everywhere in the fields with less maintenance effort and at a reasonable cost.

Fundamental dilemma (present solution): On peak need, the more you push the asset, the less reliable and consistent it becomes (injuries, weaker immune system). Also, increasing the power by adding horses, makes consistent progress difficult due to different performance between individual horses.

Important connections: The wider ploughing device, the fewer passes.

2   Go extreme
Fuel energized engine can be chosen to the desired strength and can supply this power consistently as long as there is enough fuel, oil and air. The idea is to add a wide ploughing device onto an engine and some wheels.

3   Upscale
The current concept is meant to help plowing. But if an engine is introduced on a farm, can it be used for other things as well (first scale-up: to the entire farm)? Perhaps it can be used for reaping, digging, transporting heavy loads, lifting. All these require different machine interfaces – perhaps it would be better to create a standard power outlet and tool connection points to allow the different interfaces to use the same engine. The concept is updated.

But can other farms use the device too (second scale-up: to other farms)? Texas is quite flat, but other farms can have quite steep terrain. In this case our product needs to be quite stable, preferably wide and long with a low center of gravity. Pulling heavy things uphill on slippery ground may require the ability to pull on all the wheels.

Could other industries use a device like this (third scale-up: to other industries)?

Portfolio example

The Plug and Abandon challenge
One of the major challenges within offshore oil and gas production is how to safely and effectively plug wells after their commercial lifetime is over. Although this may sound like a trivial challenge, the effort and cost associated with this task is huge. On the Norwegian Continental Shelf for example, between 2000 and 3000 wells need to be plugged and more are being drilled every day. Traditional plugging takes in the range of about 40 days to plug using an expensive drilling rig. Under these circumstances plugging the 2000–3000 wells comes with an accumulated cost in the range of 50 billion US dollars[14]. On the bright side the potential to reduce this cost is high. As a Radical Innovation group, we took it upon ourselves to help solve this challenge and bring the cost down to a fraction of the prospective cost at the time. I'd like to share this story as an example of how we approach such a task as an innovation group.

The first thing we needed was information about the challenge. We had quite a bit of knowledge internally in the group, which is a great advantage. Still, we brought in additional expertise from outside the group to top up our own, particularly on the governmental requirements for such plugs and the process of installing plugs in order to meet or exceed the requirements. During the discussion around understanding the task at hand, a few overall directions started to emerge.

- In order to reduce the cost to a fraction, we could not twist and tweak the current process, but come up with a totally new plugging concept (so we didn't need to analyze the current situation).
- The majority of the cost was associated to the drilling rig rental. Efforts to eliminate the need of expensive rigs would be really helpful.
- Clearing room for the plug was more time consuming and therefore more costly than setting the plug itself, so parts of the new solution

had to be clearing room. Two different ways of clearing room were traditionally applied, both unpredictable in their own ways.

- ○ Milling a section away
- ○ Making a cut below the area intended for the plug and pulling everything from that point up on deck for dismantling

- Outside the first steel tubular there are often some relatively small hydraulic control lines. These lines or pipes would represent a potential leak through the plug if left complete and undamaged, so they need to be "neutralized" somehow to achieve a plug meeting requirement.

As the knowledge sharing progressed, ideas started to emerge. In the beginning these were of the wilder type that would certainly cut the time to a fraction, and some also elegantly providing a solid plug at the same time. These principles included explosives and melting under extreme temperatures. However, common to all these solutions was the lack of process control through central parts of the operation. The release of so much energy over such a short time was believed to have limited predictability and repeatability. We therefore continued to search for solutions we considered better suited for the challenge at hand.

One of the team members showed up in an innovation meeting on the current topic with an enthusiasm level way above normal. On the way to work a traffic signpost design had merged with the P&A challenge, and a new possibility was born. The signpost was made out of three extruded aluminum profiles put in a triangular shape. However, before mounting the three plates together, a pattern of cuts was machined into the plate and a force was exerted onto each side pulling the cuts open to form a simple truss work pattern (see Figure 14).

Figure 14 The signpost principle which brought the P&A challenge further (right: pre-slotted piece of plate (as extruded), Middle: Slotted plate (post machining), Left: slotted and pulled plate where the truss works structure can be recognized).

The idea merging the signpost concept and the P&A challenge was the thought that a part of the steel casing could be slotted in a similar manner and, as such, made *predictably* weaker (but not loose) and another part of casing could be cut free and parked inside the weakened part. In this way steel casing could be removed without either having to pull all casing from below the plug zone and up to the rig or having to mill away the entire casing section through the intended plug zone in the brutal way milling is, or at least be performed down hole at the time (see Portfolio example: Down hole milling center on page 14). After a short discussion, another slot pattern was proposed as an alternative to the truss work pattern. Since the truss work pattern expands, a non-slotted part of the casing can be parked inside the slotted part. The alternative pattern was a continuous helical slot allowing the parking of the slotted segment to be parked inside a non-slotted part. In addition, the helical version could be rotated one way to reduce its average diameter and ease the entry, while rotation in the opposite direction would lock further movement, all of which might be useful in an operative setting.

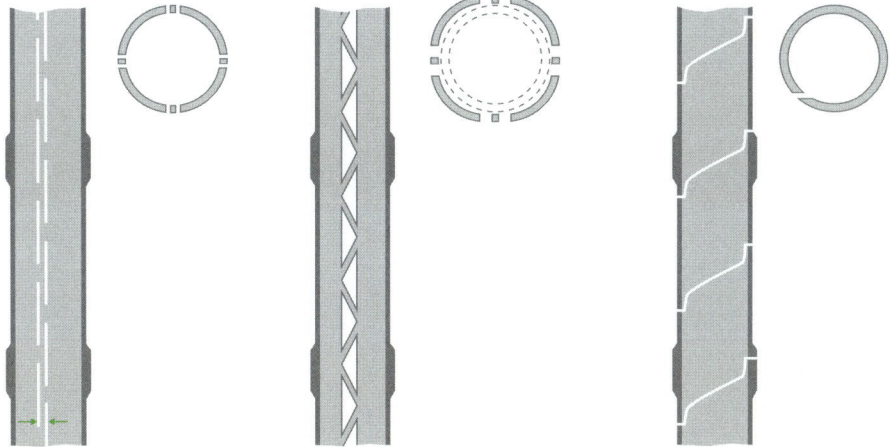

Figure 15 The signpost pattern shown unexpanded (left) and expanded (middle) and the helix shaped alternative cut (right).

Quick testing was needed to start the learning process. As an instant test specimen, we got hold of a few samples of cylindrical shaped protective hard paper housing around some large posters, which were left to collect dust in an old basement storage. With some scissors and knives, these became excellent examples of slotted casings, and the first experiments were under way. The testing went brilliantly. We quickly understood that both versions would face trouble cutting slots through the threaded connections between two tubular joints.

The signpost design was somewhat more complicated to test using paper then the helical one, so to build some useful experience also on that concept, we decided to print both designs out as rapid prototypes in plastic. This also required drawings, which is another great way to pick up useful knowledge. The rapid prototypes were excellent ways to test the two concepts and particularly to demonstrate our proposal to others. Rapid prototypes are somewhat like showing up with a puppy in public – you get easier attention and an obvious subject to initiate conversation. However, rapid prototypes do not only bring about attention, though – they also offer useful learning. The helical plastic model had to be manually modified with a file in order to work properly. Playing around with these models for a while led us to favor the signpost design to the helical one due to the smoothness of the action and the post parking capacity to hold the pipes in parked position. It was clear that the length of the slots and the distance between two slot pairs would define how heavy the parking action would be and how well they would adhere to each other afterwards due to the strain and spring back in the deformed material. From detailed drawings we saw that the number of slot pairs around the pipe perimeter would define how much the double walled steel casing diameter would increase after the parking action (see the round shape in the middle sketch in Figure 15) – the more cuts, the slimmer post parking outer diameter, which is important since this space is confined.

But drawings and models would only bring us so far. Stakeholders were supportive and comfortably curious after status updates and we were allowed to progress. Full scale testing was next – or at least testing of about 0.5 m lengths of real tubulars pulled from real wells. We made a deal with a local machine shop who could not only prepare the samples but also had a hydraulic press we could park the "sign-post" slotted pipes over non-slotted pieces of the same tubular. We performed several tests and got some numbers on parking force and how it would vary in different tribological conditions from dry to lubricated. We also studied different slot designs. We even tried a third design, proposed by one of the operators operating the press in the machine shop. He proposed one longitudinal cut through the whole parking zone – rather like the helical design, just with a straight cut. Didn't work so well for several reasons, but I think it is worth mentioning as an example of how real testing not only answers what you try to accomplish (hopefully), but also kicks off your curiosity and makes you almost subconsciously think about alternatives and improvements. Besides bringing good fun and excitement, testing is really useful to search within the solution space. And it does certainly not have to be expensive to be useful.

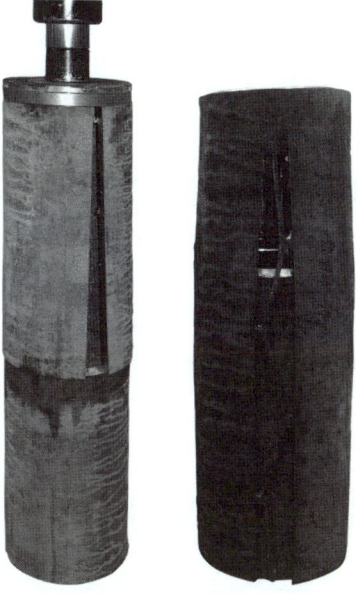

Figure 16 Pictures of the tests made on short cuts of real sized casing. The signpost design (right) and the alternative design proposed during the testing (left).

Anyway, successful tests and more updates amongst a growing interest group brought about a technical concern – would the available space between the parked casing and the next size casing be sufficiently large to accommodate the slotted liner? This was particularly a concern for those cases where this space could have quite significant control lines (hydraulic pipes for actuators etc.) within the same limited space. As facilitator I did calculations, made drawings, and reported all to our innovation group, where we became convinced that this would work. However, there was always the uncertainty around how these lines would behave jammed up in a confined space. We went for a new test with our friends in the machine shop. This time we went for a three meters long slotted real pipe to be parked over a six meters long none slotted version of itself inside a six meters real pipe of the next size. The next size pipe not only served as a realistic boundary condition for the test defining the confined space, but also served as a safety barrier against any failure that might occur. In the test we added a piece of the largest control line package I have ever seen. The control line was held in place by original clamps for that purpose. The current assembly was very near real gear in a real well, although temperature, pressure and the fluid environment was different. The amazing team in the machine shop, who wouldn't give in to anything less than basic laws of physics (and hardly also then), found an excellent and safe site in their back yard to perform the full-scale parking test.

Here the larger safety pipe was firmly bolted to a concrete wall. The force was provided by some heavy steel ballast blocks and a heavy-duty mobile crane. What a great day for innovation that was!

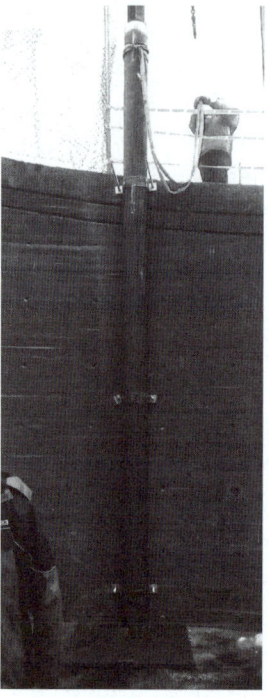

Figure 17 Pictures of the test setup (left), the end result with the control line package (upper right) and the three layers of pipe (lower right).

The deformation was as smooth as could be. The forces were as expected or even lower. Post testing the parked assembly was brought down, disassembled and cut open to inspect the parking function and the control line behavior in the now-so-famous confined space. This had neatly folded up within the available space and was neither ruptured nor a significant hindrance for the parking process. We could proceed to report a successful test.

As an innovation team, we considered the concept proven and felt that the project was ready to be proposed to relevant stakeholders. The main stakeholder in this case was organizationally one level higher than the representative who had followed the project from the department holding the P&A mandate within research. To our surprise we discovered that they didn't like the milling part, and pointed out that this would take longer than we had anticipated. There were some concerns about this method's applicability on certain special casing design cases as well. Cutting connections were also considered too risky. Our concept was simply found not to be good enough as presented. What a day *that* was for innovation.

When a river encounters an obstacle, it will gather in deeper and deeper concentration until a new way is found.

Anyway, our innovation group decided to make a new attempt to further optimize the concept. As usual, during the new ideation session several options surfaced, but ended up with the ambition to check out if cutting could be done using high pressure water cutting with abrasives, just like the machine shop had done making the slots on our full scale test (see Figure 18). As facilitator I spent time after the session searching realistic data, designing feasible task sequences and calculating time saved, consumable volumes and other relevant information with which we could convince ourselves and others of the supremacy of our new update. In the process I also discovered that both abrasive water jetting and hydraulic jacking, which were the two main operating methods applied in this configuration, had been used in down hole situations already, although separately. Estimations indicated significant time saving as many slots could be cut simultaneously around the perimeter using a specially designed tool for the job. Three thousand wells could arguably justify such a specialized tool. The tool would be a combination of a hydraulic jack with two anchors in each end and a jetting slide (like can be seen in Patent No. GB2534546). This tool would cut, pull and park a casing segment of about six meters in one anchor setting – all on wireline, reducing the vessel size requirement dramatically. Estimations indicated that by repeating this action nine times, it could open the necessary space for a plug in 27 hours including tripping, using a small vessel.

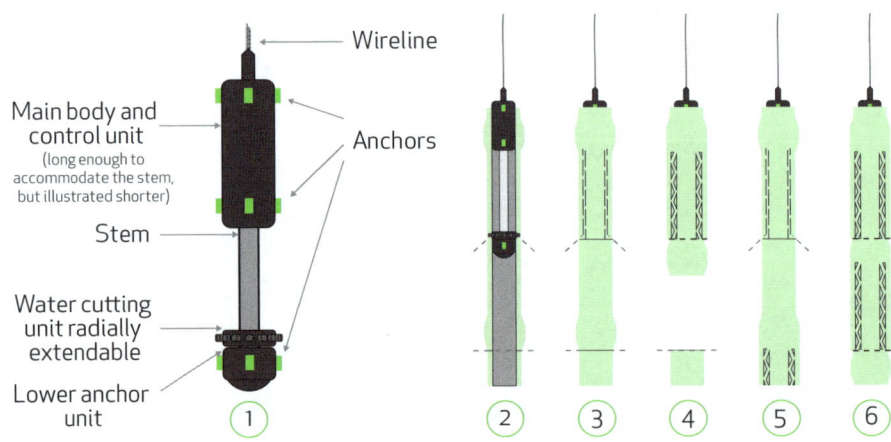

Figure 18 The last version including water jetting the slots. The tool and its components (1) and examples of how the tool works (2–6). The tool inside the pipe after cutting loose the section to be parked (2), outside view of the slotted receiver of the first section to be parked (3), first section parked (4), cut the second section (including the first section in parked state (5) and second section parked (6).

We approached the main stakeholders again. Despite the later improvements, the decision was to continue prioritizing the already ongoing efforts on P&A until further notice, and this is also the status at the moment of writing.

This Plug and Abandon story is just one example of many developments our group has created over the years. Out of our quite wide portfolio, I share a few examples relevant to the subject being discussed at various parts of the book. Other concept examples in headline format include:

- A low wear choke valve where no sealing surfaces are exposed during normal use
- Two concepts reducing the weight (and cost) of offshore wind turbines
- Several new field development methods for marginal fields
- Low CO_2 gas compression
- Low CO_2 gas turbine
- Floating wind turbine for specific tasks offshore
- Walk2work bridge between two floating installations
- A new thread system to save time and assure quality making up threaded connections
- More effective purchasing system for procurement
- Robust and low maintenance multi-flow measurement tool
- Fully automatized drilling rig at a fraction of an equivalent standard rig size
- Autonomous inflow control device separating water and hydrocarbons before they enter the well
- Noise reduction on a process plant.

Unfortunately, the most interesting examples cannot be shared in detail due to confidentiality reasons. They will have to wait for a later occasion.

What works and what does not in a radical innovation group

This section outlines some of the knowledge of what works well and what could be wise to avoid, based on years of experience running such radical innovation groups.

Live performance

The value of live performance should not be underestimated. Information exchange like presentations, verbal verifications, concrete questions and such can take place via video conferences, phone calls and the like, and still provide valuable contributions. However, creative work happens best in physical meetings where all the participants are physically present. Creativity drops dramatically when anyone in the group connects remotely – at least with classic technology. Modern tools to share sound, images and work interface like a sketch/drawing board, compensate for some of this inconvenience, but they cannot fully compensate for the inter-human level, which is so important for creativity in my opinion. I do, however, recognize that remote connections can be helpful during the brain storming phase of creative sessions due to the fact that participants can feel more protected and distant during their perceived exposure when rather wild ideas are brought forward "in public".

Care must be taken when guests with expertise are invited to the group in order to extend the knowledge base. The quality level of the guest is likely to increase if remote contact is possible simply because there are more people from which to choose. On the other hand, the quality of the interaction with the radical innovation group will decrease at the same time. Information exchange will probably be good, but the knowledge transfer part of the meeting will gradually change into a creative session in which the expert will play an important role. In this part, nothing outcompetes physical presence.

Shepherd leadership and framing the search

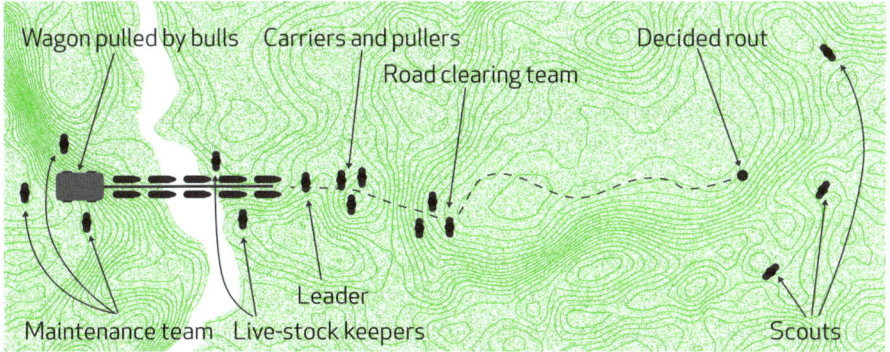

The facilitator is and should be an active part of the group with the same authority level as the others. The facilitator should NOT take the role of a traditional leader. Leadership leads, makes decisions, goes in front and shows the way. The reason is that leadership comes with responsibility. The leadership is responsible for the actions of everyone below them. To manage this responsibility, rules and best practice are put in place accompanied by verification systems verifying that the rules actually are followed. In addition, companies have things like Key Performance Indicators and different personal goal distribution systems to make sure that everyone pulls in the same direction. This is Alignment Leadership and is suitable for production and operative type of environments where tasks are repetitive and needs prequalification to assure correct effect. As an example, you don't want the pilot to try out some cool new innovative moves when landing your plane.

However, Alignment Leadership is inefficient when it comes to innovation[13] and in particular when it comes to radical innovation. Let's look at a metaphoric example. You have the task to bring a large heavy component in a wagon through a part of the jungle a few hundred years ago, at the time before motorized vehicles where available (see illustration above). You would obviously need a lot of strong pulling animals, like horses and/or bulls, and a lot of people assisting you. If this is a "one time" occasion, you would probably not just start the whole procession and handle issues as they arise. Turning the procession around in front of a canyon would be somewhere between seriously inefficient and impossible. In unknown territory like this you would typically send out some scouts. Their mission would be to draw you a map and point out the best route for a procession pulling a heavy wagon. You would give them the general direction you need to go (the frame) and let them search for the best option to get there. You would not give them detailed instructions where to search, because you want every possibility examined (not risk based progress evaluation). If they reported a canyon (a failure), you would deeply appreciate the contribution and make sure to put it clearly on the map. If the pioneers found a fairly decent route, you would like them to continue the search hoping to discover an even better alternative, since you know that some extra pioneer time may greatly save total effort. Only when the map is clear for the first stage, would you mobilize the procession. On the other hand, for the procession, you would give clear instructions on where to go and how to work, have risk based evaluation on changes and measure progress, or in other words; *traditional or alignment leadership*.

Ideation and early phase innovation work are like the pioneers. It is about searching new territory and drawing up the map. It is about celebrating failures, learning, sharing and moving on. It is about not being satisfied with fairly good, but searching further for excellence, because the effort at this stage is so cheap compared to commercialization and production that it is worth spending the extra time. And it is about the upper leadership giving the general overall direction; *the frame*, and let the team search freely within the frame (see Figure 19). This is *framed search*.

The fundamental difference between the two ways of leading is that alignment leadership requires the leadership to know where to go and to have tested that the way is fit for purpose, while innovation leadership and framing is needed when the route is not known. But how can we assure that framed search is safe, like the tested route and rules of alignment leadership. Well, ideas start in the head and proceed to lines on paper or a blackboard. A major mistake doesn't physically harm anyone (but rather offers a good laugh). Next stage, testing things in a lab, has a harm potential. So here care must be taken. But initial testing is normally simple, so with low damage potential and proper safety measures, risk can be mitigated quite easily allowing the search to be free in the real sense of the word. Many companies define the maturity of a technology on a scale from an idea all the way through to the implemented product (technology readiness level). *Framed search* is the leadership model on the idea side of the scale and traditional *alignment leadership* is on the implemented product's side, with a gradual transition between. Brilliant leaders manage this transition uninterruptedly in the various situations they meet during the day (see also *Building an innovative culture amongst the Idea Receivers* staring on page 184 for more on this subject).

Radical innovation is about searching an unknown area for new possibilities in pioneer style. The best solutions may well lie in a direction that initially appears like a clear dead end. A good facilitator of a radical innovation group defines clearly within which area the search will take place and allows the whole team to make the search freely. Framing the search in this way is very important to focus attention and be targeted. The base frame is the business or customer need, as explained in the More about on page 56. The need represents an excellent frame for an innovative process. The business or customer need can however be large, too large as a stated challenge for a good innovative session. However, the need can be divided into subgroups, which make up excellent innovation challenges. For example if we want to meet the need: "Provide every person on earth with their daily need for food", this can be divided into different sub-groups like one for providing food for people in Africa and one for people in North America, two groups that probably require a very different approach. The frame doesn't necessarily have to be the need itself or parts of it. A frame can also be one or several stepping-stones on a road that eventually would lead to a fulfilled need. In our "food for all" example, one frame that would make up a very good innovation challenge could be: "How to double the food production?" and another: "How to efficiently distribute nutrition rich food?" The food production frame can yet again be divided into for example: "How to double the effective outcome per planted acreage?" or: "How to effectively make use of otherwise wasted food?" In this way a major need can be divided into manageable innovation challenges as a frame for a group session. The facilitator organizes a systematic approach through all these frames so that the end result, the sum of all the work, actually meets the intended need. And for radical innovation, the overall need should stay bold and ambitious to avoid ending up on the incremental track. Therefore, I usually start with a large frame to get the overview and find overarching dependencies and opportunities. Then we try to keep the predominant insight as we explore smaller more specific frames to avoid sub-optimization.

Overarching insight vs. sub-optimization is important. There is always a danger associated with dividing the need into smaller sub-needs. The more division, the more you accept the structure of the division and the more difficult it is to find solutions beyond that structure, which in turn means we approach a more incremental outcome of our effort. Let's again look at the "food for all" example, where we proposed to divide into efficient production and efficient transport. The transport bit could easily be divided into efficient sea transport and land transport, the land transport again into developing world transport and industrialized world transport, and so on. The more we divide the more we distance ourselves from real radical solutions where production and transport are one, or where transport is not needed (local production for example). See also *Horse example* on page 60 and how analyses may have resulted in incremental results and led the focus away from the tractor. Generally radical innovation takes zooming out, and not zooming in. The only reason to zoom in is if the task seems too large for a fruitful session, like "food for all" might be for many.

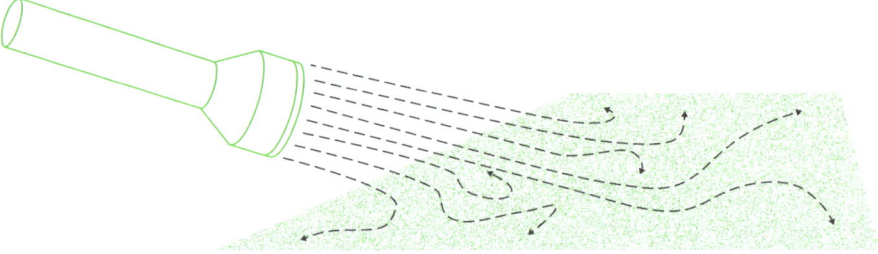

Figure 19 Illustration of a frame defining the innovation task. There is free search within the frame where the objective is to explore as much as possible, but the search does not extend beyond the frame.

It is also worth mentioning that it can be quite complicated to get a clear, broad understanding of a need. A full understanding of the need requires an understanding of the implications for every part involved in the value chain, every interface, every angle and even down to every feeling a customer or user might have. As an example, let us again look at the "food for all" example and the frame, "how to efficiently distribute nutrition rich food?" Obviously, we must stretch to attend to the needs of the people who so desperately need this food to get a meaningful life. But we should also strive to attend to the needs of, for example, the transporter, the loader, the economic benefit of the transporting company (= their business need), the environmental impact, the experience of the people directly or indirectly affected by the transport on issues like sound effects, visual appearance, local air pollution considerations, traffic flow, employment, regulations and much more. The overall need is a sum of all these needs, and the best solutions incorporate all. There are several techniques to develop well-articulated realistic need statements, one of which is commonly referred to as *Design Thinking*. Design thinking is based on empathizing the considerations around the customer and the user. It is not this book's aim to train people in these techniques, other than convincing as many as possible that this type of needs represents excellent starting points for innovation in the form of frames for the search.

When a frame is in place, communicated and understood, whether it is the need itself or a sub-division of the need, the facilitator's role turns more into a team supporter function. The facilitator can assist the search by supportive analyses or provide objective knowledge. However, the facilitator (or any other person in a leading position for that matter), does not decide which solution to pursue and which to abandon. The group decides together which ideas to pursue further, and this could be one or several. Even if only one member is behind a certain idea, it should be pursued because this individual may have seen something the others have not. It is all about drawing the map of the unexplored territory within the given frame. The next stage is testing, and that may (or may not) reduce the number of candidates. *Objective tests are the best way to determine the quality of an idea and not a person's gut-feeling or intuition.* Remember that a failing test is also a contribution to the map construction, and should therefore be considered positive. Obviously somewhere within that frame we believe the best solution for commercialization can be found. In order to find out if a solution candidate really is the best, you need to know all other possibilities to be confident, also those that do not work. The sooner you find out, the cheaper and therefore also the better it is. Exploring the frame is the time to celebrate failure.

Nelson Mandela said, "A leader is like a shepherd. He stays behind the flock letting the most nimble go out ahead whereupon the others just follow, not realizing that all along they are being directed from behind."

 Targeted innovation is free search within clear frames.

To see framing illustrated in a larger context, see Figure 27.

Company management and leadership as radical group members

From a competence point of view, we have seen that a good radical team member has a wide (shallow) knowhow around his/her expertise (see *Core group members* on page 46). To be promoted to management and leadership, the selected individual has often stood out from the rest of their fellow employees as someone possessing particular skills to get that opportunity, whether it is special knowledge or certain behavioral skills. In addition, management and leadership normally interact with more activities both closer and more remote to their own area of responsibility in their duty as front-runners than an employee does. Such front-runners are therefor likely to have a wider knowhow than normal in addition to an expertise, both of which make them good candidates for radical innovation groups. Other skills must also be considered, of course. A particularly important skill for this specific group of candidates in radical innovation context is their ability to leave their "distinctions" outside the room and participate on the same level as all the rest – this is indeed a prerequisite for participation (see previous paragraph).

Focus on possible Showstoppers

While exploring new possible radical concepts, it is always a question about which obstacles to worry about and which not to worry about until later. To answer this question, it could be useful to think about how an idea develops from its infancy into a developed innovation. I have yet to come across an idea that has not changed during this bumpy development road. The probability of change depends on the level of detail. Normally the main intention survives, although even that may change (in which case one can argue that it is now a new idea). All other aspects on a lower detail level stand the chance of scrutiny and change. The more detailed the concept aspect is, the higher the probability of change is and the expected number of times it will change increases accordingly. This is why details should receive a low focus in the ideation phase. And even more importantly, any evaluation of early stage ideas needs to disregard the details. What would the logic be to stop an idea at an evaluation gate due to something that will change soon anyway (see *Building an innovative culture amongst the Idea Receivers* on page 184)? Therefore, the evaluation focus in the early stages of the innovation process should be on possible *Showstoppers*, given that the idea is within the frames of the search and can add value. A Showstopper is anything that can make it impossible to develop and implement the concept, like aspects in conflict with the physical laws.

The importance of the room in which innovation takes place

Innovation need to physically take place somewhere. Many spend a lot of time and resources to make advanced and well-equipped facilities to meet the innovator's needs. I don't think this is strictly necessary. Again, we can start off very simple, in a good Lean Startup spirit. In the following it could be useful to separate the discussion between where imaginative work takes place and where testing takes place.

A place where imaginative work takes place can be very simple. However, it should look different from classic meeting rooms in the company – first and foremost for the invitees to immediately sense that the session they are invited to also differs from a standard meeting. One of the differences can be fewer and less comfortable seats. Innovation in action is a dynamic process where people move and shares spaces like the drawing board and the computer where information is sought and presented. During really good sessions, chairs have a tendency to get in the way, and so do large tables. The room can advantageously have many places to draw, where the group can share sketches. It is also important to have the possibility to seek information to be shared in a place where all can view it. In addition, it can be useful to have places where models, posters and informative material can be surrounded by the candidates when an aspect needs everyone's attention, although this is not strictly necessary. Such a room is simple and not particularly expensive since many of the changes we have done to a more classic meeting room is to move things out.

A testing place can also be simple. An empty garage-type room can be enough, or a place where the inventors can come to after having passed by the local hardware store or whatever is available to buy simple things to build the first prototype. However, in the case of a test facility, it would in fact add value if the available equipment became more sophisticated. This can be computer-based drawing and mathematical simulation systems, installations for machining, additive manufacturing capabilities and more. But these are not strictly necessary. A lot of excellent innovation has started under very simple conditions.

A good test facility would obviously serve as a good room to stretch your imagination, however, a simple test place will not be counterproductive and may bring you far.

Acceptance of failure

Someone once said: "If you never fall while skiing, you don't push yourself enough". And there is a lot to that saying. If you don't push yourself, you don't learn and eventually you don't improve. Within innovation learning is key. A negative result can be as valuable as a positive one when we explore and pioneer our way through the frame defining our task at hand (see Figure 19). All results guide us further and provide valuable experience on the way (see also the metaphor in *Shepherd leadership and framing the search* on page 85). In my experience you need to fail a number of times and make appropriate adjustments before a success can be born. In an innovative group, a dead-end triggers more energy, which is then focalized on how to get around the issue responsible for the dead-end. In this light, failure is a necessary part of success. There is a lot in Nelson Mandela's words: "I never lose – I either win or learn".

The real challenge with failures will probably not come from within the group. Innovative groups learn quickly to appreciate any data point, including the failures. Stakeholders around innovative groups who may spend most of their day in a less innovative environment can have less patience with failures and dead-ends. This is important to keep in mind when setting up the organizational structure around the radical innovation groups. It is also important for the radical innovation group to keep this potential attitude in mind when communicating results outside the group.

It is indeed fundamental for an innovation group to have the freedom to search within the frame. With free search comes failures. If there is a fear of failures, the probability for success falls dramatically. Building an acceptance of a failure culture both inside and outside the group is therefore very important.

When to be supportive and when not to be

The main purpose for a radical innovation group in action is to build viable concepts of a different nature. All the methods and techniques in this chapter are about facilitating this process. Two very central elements in this process are to suggest an idea (metaphorically: plant a seed) and to build the idea to a convincing concept (make the seed grow). It should come as no surprise to anyone that predominately a supportive attitude is necessary to build this skillset, as a group, and regularly develop good innovative concepts of a radical nature time and time again. But the question is how critical we can allow ourselves to be to each other within the group. Some say that it is not allowed to be negative at all to ideas or proposals. I think this is counterproductive and one can end up spending much time on ideas that are clearly out of scope. Negativity is indeed allowed, but certain principles apply.

First of all, I have never felt the need to emphasize which ideas to scrap. In a good innovative meeting, a lot of ideas should surface. The best will naturally grow and gain necessary support. Certain group members may advocate less obvious ideas, which may well prove to be great at a later stage; these also should continue into the testing stage. All the rest has now been indirectly scrapped without an explicit ditch statement. In a way the jungle law applies; the best survive and the others will rest in peace. But resting ideas can be brought up again at a later stage, perhaps in a different setting. In other words, scrapping ideas can take place without critical statements.

However, sometimes critical and negative statements are necessary. Some claim this is one of the fundamental roles of such a group (see More about below on page 95). When a critical and negative statement is necessary, make sure these are followed by a reasonable, factual and convincing argumentation, and never built on gut-feeling alone. Also, it could be a good idea to delay these statements to make sure you have fully understood the proposal and made sure that no one else has picked it up to go in a more viable direction. Remember that poor ideas can be important steppingstones for great ideas. It is also a great advantage if critical or negative statements are followed by new and supposedly improved statements of the type "I think this part is great, but I am not sure that this part here would work because… How about turning this part here around instead like this… to achieve an even larger…?"

Critical comments can cause some friction in the group and some heat in the discussions. Within reasonable limits and with respect, friction may well be a good thing creating energy and ultimately new solutions.

Finally, it goes without saying that critical and negative statements should address ideas and proposals, and not the individual who articulates them, nor should these be made to enhance the relative importance of other ideas on the table.

More about...

...different roles in a radical innovation group.
In the core of a creative process, in the phase were the ideation takes place, we often see that the different participants take different roles[20]. These roles can be changed from time-to-time, from case-to-case and even from discussion-to-discussion. The most normal roles are the

1. Creative
2. Critical
3. Knowledgeable

It is natural that the one proposing an idea takes the creative role as the defending party, although it is not automatically like this. Someone else will soon pick up the critical role. The critical roles objective is to search for and ask questions about anything associated with complications and doubt, with the ultimate objective to shed light over the entire suggestion and smoke out fundamental problems early in order to build and find new ways. Particularly, the critical role must be done with caution and social skills. Being critical is a balance between finding the weak spots and maintaining the positive upwards spiral.

With these two roles, the creative and the critical, the stage is all set for an explorative discussion. This is the minimum configuration to be productive. One role can be held by several individuals.

Very often a third role enters the stage – the knowledgeable. This is typically the one who sits on most knowledge about the field being discussed at any time. And interestingly enough in itself, often suggestions come from people with a distance to the knowledge. This role will often be more neutral to the outcome and be more focused on providing objective information.

Where to find inspiration and get ideas

The world is indeed facing many challenges, but there are even more solutions out there, solutions ready to yet again form the basis of new concepts solving new or even old challenges. We have spoken about how systematic innovative efforts with advantages can start with a need (see More about on page 56). But when the need is clear, where to search for inspiration and solutions?

To start, let us look into the inspiration part. One place to start is *megatrends*. Megatrends are major movements we see over time in large parts of the world. These are contemporary trends like digitalization, robotization, urbanization, CO_2 efficient energy creation and many more. To look closer at these and discover many more, simply perform a net-search on the word "megatrends" and your screen will be full of relevant information. This book is about radical innovation, so don't accept these megatrends uncritically. Perhaps your new solution can be found in a brand-new trend breaking with these megatrends, challenging them all together. Or oppositely, perhaps the megatrends can help shape a credible future scenario for your specific challenge. Nevertheless, these type of massive long-term movements can inspire new thinking.

Another way, or perhaps even a continuation of the megatrends, is to stretch into extreme situations. With digitalization and robotization is mind, you can ask yourself how to solve the challenge at hand without any manual interference at all, perhaps adding "in a lifecycle perspective" to make it all more challenging. Or how can your need be met without any CO_2 created? Quite on the contrary, could we also search for a decentralized solution, directly counteracting the urbanization trend, and see how the future scenario would look then. Extreme challenges call for extreme solutions that can inspire less extreme and more rational solutions in a shorter time perspective.

Yet another probably more commonly applied way to find inspiration would be to look at other industries normally known to be further in their development level on the current topic than yourself. For example, if you are producing traditional ventilation systems and you want to make your process more efficient, you may search for inspiration at car manufacturers, who have taken the assembly line technology and the just in time principles really far. The difference between these two manufacturing processes are large and solutions are not readily transferable, but it can be a great place to seek inspiration to find your own improvement points. And perhaps the car industry could pick up an interesting aspect or two from you, too, in which case both could come out stronger from the initiative.

However, inspiration is not enough. We need real solutions from which we build up a new real concept of a viable nature. Let us take the invention of a classic light bulb as example. We are back in year 1850 or so and have been inspired by the contemporary megatrend electrification. We would like to provide people with electric light instead of the light shed from something burning directly, like candles. In retrospect we know that the electric light bulb will be an important trade item for another 160 years or so, which is quite encouraging for our quest. But a great part of innovation remains. How to accomplish a light bulb someone will spend their hard-earned cash to buy? For the purpose of this discussion, it could be useful to separate the solution space into basic research on one hand and commercial product generation on the other, created by respectively scientists and innovators. Scientists can obviously also be innovators (and vice versa), but not necessarily. An integral part of innovation is commercialization. A scientist can discover important breakthroughs without actually commercializing them. Fundamental research is an example. So back to our quest for the light bulb. To come up with the light bulb we need to borrow work from those who came up with glass and their technique to shape it into a light bulb shape. We need electricity knowledge from those who developed that, skills on metal, how to shape it and knowledge about its behavior when glowingly hot. We also need to know about inert gasses and their extreme properties. All of these are indispensable building blocks for a light bulb. Each building block serves a purpose, so only when you understand each building block and how they interrelate to make up the totality (the light bulb), will a new solution be borne. If it is commercially attractive, the solution also becomes viable.

Therefore, after the inspiration, innovation is about assembling a new set of building blocks making up a commercially viable totality. Promising building blocks are all around us all the time, from those simple ones in daily life to those less available at the sharp end of basic research at any given time. I have noticed that the more I do systematic radical innovation, the more I can appreciate elegant solutions that I come across in my everyday life, and try hard to store them in mind for an occasion where they come in handy. The multiskill requirement for a radical innovation group is about accessing more relevant building blocks.

Leaving the 19th century with the light bulb challenge and returning to a radical innovation setting in our times, it is interesting to look closer at the fundamental difference between open innovation with, for example, crowd sourcing on one hand and an internal radical innovation muscle similar to the one this book proposes on the other hand. With open innovation and crowd sourcing, the incoming solutions are likely to be made at a distance from the actual need, the capabilities, context and culture of the receiving part (see Figure 20). This doesn't mean that it is worthless, quite on the contrary. However, these incoming solutions are likely to be more on the building block side of the solution space. The optimal solution to our challenge may contain elements from many incoming ideas, which again need further work to be lifted from good into excellent, fulfilling the need in a manner well adapted to the current situation of the company, such as know-how, available assets, resources generally, networks, culture and so on. This is work for a radical innovation muscle. Bringing representatives from the best incoming solutions together with internal radical innovation capabilities can potentially shape, twist and tweak the available material to elevate the effort to excellence (see Figure 21).

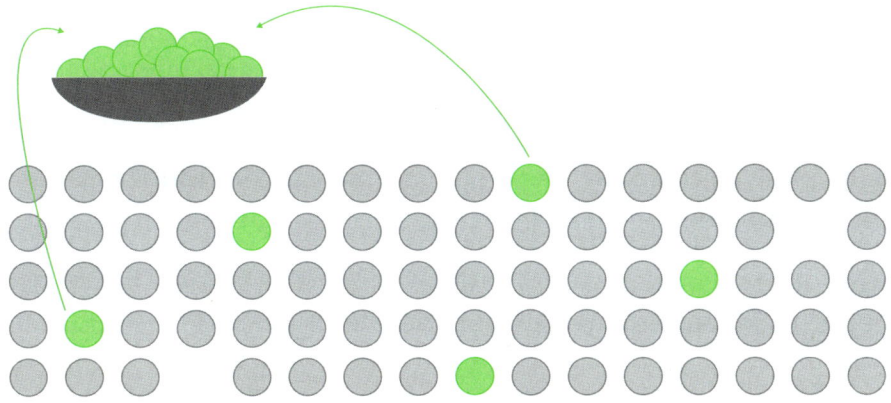

Figure 20 Crowd sourcing solutions to a challenge allows the collection of many independent ideas that can to a varying extent fit the need they were meant to cover. Further work may be needed to lift a few from good, single ideas to one excellent concept fulfilling the need.

Figure 21 Bringing together many independent ideas (from Figure 20) to mature them into a viable concept well adapted to the challenge, the capabilities, context and culture of the receiving part may require both representatives from each stand-alone idea but also internal resources to assure the local dimension.

Timing

When discussing what works and what doesn't for radical innovation it is hard to get around *timing*. So important and so hard to do right – at least repeatedly. Timing could mean the difference between success and total failure. This is particularly interesting to see in connection with competitive mind-sets, passion for innovation, progress and drive for improvement. All of the above make true innovators often want to scream out their discoveries to the world as soon as the idea is "materialized" – perhaps just as a mental image. However, at this point the red warning light named *timing* should flash to prevent the screaming part and advise you to consider the overall situation first. For the purpose of this discussion, timing can be divided into two types.

First, timing the development level at which the idea can be shared with the receiver. At what point during the development process is it wise to share with potential hand-over candidates? Will the receiver appreciate the bare idea or would it take calculations, modelling and even tests to be convincing? This varies a lot between receivers, their motivation (potential upside) and sense of urgency. Operative people who are approached as potential users and will end up with problems if things fail would typically require more mature concepts than researchers and strategy people, for example. The perceived urgency of the receiver would typically play a role, the level of benefit the idea would bring about, but also individual personality differences should be considered before deciding the maturity level needed to make the necessary impact.

Secondly, timing with respect to the total situation around the receiver can play an important role whether or not the new concept will be welcomed or not. This can be how many other options the receiver works on for this particular need and how they advance. These can be available recourses, company strategy, company stock value, the company's standing relative to their competitors and major effects like economic up or downturns for the industry segment, the region or the world.

To master the selling process of innovative concepts can be quite complicated and takes flair for timing. This is particularly the case for radical innovation. Even if the innovation was based on a clear need (see More about on page 56), the receiver may be prone to choose a low risk incremental remedy for the need, to the expense of a high value radical one. A way to maximize the probability of a sale is to go from "push" to "pull". *Push* in this setting means that the idea proposer actively seeks an idea receiver who could pursue and support the idea forward. *Pull* means that the receiver actively searches for solutions to a challenge that happens to fit the idea the proposer promotes. In a pull situation most of the timing challenges above are minimized since the initiative comes from the receiver. It is indeed convincing when a receiver asks for ideas and a proposer pulls a well-adapted concept out of the sleeve, which holds a maturity level beyond expectations. This is a really good start of a cooperation. One way to get into this position is to make an accumulation of ideas and seek arenas where ideas are sought. This takes lots of patience and self-control but may prove to be really powerful.

Later in this book, we will see how you can get a wider company focus on a concept by the use of mental anchors if a project stakeholder is on-board as a supporter (see IMPLEMENT – TAKE OUT THE FULL VALUE POTENTIAL on page 148).

Portfolio example

An example of the timing effect from our portfolio is a subsea solution worked on quite a few years ago. Unfortunately, I cannot share details about the concept in this case. Nevertheless, the concept was born on the way home from a problem-solving workshop on the issue. While the rest of the "common effort" focused on analyzing the current situation in a search for remedies that could help solve the issue, the new radical concept came out of a creative session without analyses. All analyses were put aside under the assumption that a totally new solution was needed to achieve a lasting effect. The new radically different solution shaped up as lines on paper and later pixels on screens. No mathematical modelling or testing was made. The explanation of the fundamental effects and the physical laws was clear and understandable alone.

> However, understandable was not sufficient to create enthusiasm in this case. All those with responsibility within this particular field found this solution to be far too easy and said it didn't take in the total complexity of the situation. The whole concept was parked in a drawer.
>
> Many years later the industry started to turn in exactly this direction and now this solution is common within this field. The timing of the radical concept was really poor. In retrospect, I can imagine that it would have been better to wait until the analyzing period was over, and the stakeholders would have switched over from fact-search mode to brainstorming mode. Waiting just those one-to-two years the search phase lasted could have saved five to ten years in this case.

Different methods to excellence

Is the proposed method in this book the only way to build structural strength on radical innovation in the company? Absolutely not! There are many ways to succeed and even more ways to fail in this important endeavor. Innovation is systematic curiosity, it is about multiskill and can also be about multi-method. So in fact, applying different methods can be an asset in itself giving you even more insight in the end.

Innovation is applying creativity systematically.

What characterizes the method described herein is the following:
- The cost of the effort is really low and the benefit can be huge.
- Virtual teams can start really small and yield real results relatively quickly despite the size. Remember, one small group can lay major golden eggs. The value of a concept is not proportional to group size, budget, attention span or the like – if anything, it is rather inversely proportional. Upscaling by increasing the number of groups will

increase the probability by increasing the number of results.
- With a small group you can try, adjust, try again, and if necessary, adjust yet again until you get it right for you and your environment. An initially low promotion factor can be an advantage in leaving room for adjustments without anyone "losing face" (in a culture where nobody can be seen making mistakes).
- The method is easily scalable, both in active participation, supporting functions and internal as well as external attention.
- The group's ability to combine endurance and renewal is key to maintain relevance over time. This ability is fueled by the combination of new invitees and a fixed core group with their daily activities in their respective organizational units.
- The structure is dynamic in the sense that substantial changes to the group structure can be made with a low organizational impact.
- The flat and decentralized virtual structure promotes free search, which limits the ability of specific individuals to influence the free search.
- The flat and decentralized virtual structure multiplies the involvement level throughout the company over departmental borders down to the level of individuals, even beyond the company borders if preferred. This is active innovation culture building (see *Radical innovation not only for tomorrow but also for today* on page 153).
- The Boomerang effect can reduce the high risk associated with radical innovation by promoting more efficient incremental innovation with an increased ability to adjust while advancing.

Inconveniences with this system can be:
- The dynamic structure of virtual teams makes it easy to prematurely terminate.
- The flat and decentralized virtual structure can make it difficult for management to align collective efforts (which on the other hand could also limit the innovative capacity).
- The flat and decentralized virtual structure can make efficient networking challenging.

- The virtual structure may be challenging for implementing ideas as virtual in an organizational sense, here understood as an "occasional" sub-structure across the formal organization, and makes a formal organizational mandate demanding.

106 Integrate – fit innovation groups into your organization

Chapter summary:

This chapter is about how to scale up your radical innovation efforts from Chapter 2 and integrate them into the organization. The main purpose is to provide the upper management with a variety of realistic and valuable future options in order for them to make the best strategic choices ahead of competition.

You will hear more about:

- Strengthening your radical innovation effort by duplicating the pilot innovation group, and, if successful, to duplicate again and again.
- Applying a wide group distribution strategy to drain radical suggestions from all parts of the company applying the multiskill principle not only within a group but also between radical innovation groups.
- Adding new groups to the radical innovation family in a slow and careful manner is active risk management in accordance with Eric Ries' brilliant philosophy on Lean Startup[2].
- Creating a live group network can create positive and healthy balance between competition and cooperation amongst the radical innovation groups.
- The best innovation group reporting practice, and how radical concepts should be reported to the leadership level of the company and not lower levels, to avoid sub-optimization of potentially important strategic possibilities.
- How the leadership can proactively challenge the radical groups in return in order to pursue directions they consider promising and as such motivate further targeted searching.
- How to use this theory to generate radically different results also in a workshop setting with people normally not involved in systematic radical innovation work.
- How to use this theory as a project management tool to create agility and alignment throughout the project.

Build a network of radical innovation groups

After a serious effort over time to build a radical innovation pilot group (the subject of the previous chapter), your company should have a well-functioning radical innovation group, and you should start to see the contours of *value for money*. The effort spent is merely a few hours by the group members a week and a few quick tests occasionally. The investment is certainly low. The direct value added is hopefully a critical view of the present business and several realistic and perhaps also exiting new valuable propositions, or let's say *options* for the future. Next chapter will detail out how these possibilities or options can bring significant value to the present business too in a short time perspective, long before the radical concept has been implemented. Another more indirect value of the radical innovation pilot is the effect on the general innovation culture, which is constantly working consciously or subconsciously in the background. Bringing people normally not in interaction together in meaningful innovation work on a regular basis will spread the innovation spirit and the belief that innovative success actually is possible when returning to their own environments as well. "Across silo activities" are valuable in themselves – the larger the company, the more vital. If the total value of your radical innovation group is evident and acceptable, it is time to scale up the effort, which this chapter is all about.

If value creation is not evident, it may be a good idea to revisit and evaluate the pilot and see if anything can be improved. This is well in line with the principles brought forward by Erik Ries[2] and his concept Lean Startup. He argues that one should not plan and develop the perfect product before rolling things out to the customer. Instead and quite on the contrary, one should create a *minimum viable product* and go out as soon as possible to test it in real life on real customers in order to get early realistic and valuable "customer" feed-back. This is exactly the purpose of the first radical innovation group. Start small with low cost. Through real experience I am *really* convinced that this effort will pay off if the principles listed in this book are more or less followed. We are far from exact science here, and the process is robust. Quite significant deviations from the content between these two covers may well lead to positive results. The reason for my sincere conviction is that I have experienced how the efforts listed in Chapter 2 really produce radical innovation. Radical innovation is perceived by many as a process crossing the border to coincidence and well on the way to magic, but it can really be a systematic process capable of generating high quality results on a regular basis. If you do not get value for money in this effort after having given the pilot enough time for the participants to get familiarized with each other and the process, then scrutinize the effort, make adjustments and try again. There is really no magic, but a question of following the model (see Figure 27).

Radical innovation is a result of systematic hard work and not magic.

When you see that the pilot does yield value, it is time to scale the effort up. Strategy work and the future are far too important to leave in the hands of a few people, or even worse, to coincidence, which stopping the effort might do. The objective should be to supply strategy work with realistic, concrete and feasible ideas and concepts presented in a visual way from many places in the company and even beyond.

Initiate a new group, similar to the effort creating the pilot. Build up slowly, give the effort some time, evaluate and if needed adjust. Connect the two groups and let them inspire and challenge each other. With this connection a network for radical innovation is born. At this point it is important to be conscious about how successes from each group are rewarded. If the regime is, "the best wins", the competitive spirit is neutered but the cooperation environment is heavily affected in a negative way. The most important is the collective creativity, and this is a result of cooperation and sharing. On the other hand, if the regime is instead, "all useful suggestions are rewarded and everyone involved shares", the competitive level may not reach as high, but the important cooperation part will strengthen. The groups will be composed differently by different individuals with different insights and qualities. Working on the same challenge individually, the chance is that the two groups will end up with differences in their solutions. In the same way as different suggestions from two individuals within a group can play off each other better and even kick-start a third solution outcompeting the two originals, constructive dialogue on results between groups may well lead to more than the sum of the input. Preserving this positive cooperation dimension can really grow and shape systematic concept construction. Concepts may be composed by numbers of ideas from anywhere in the company, which when individually isolated may classify more as wishful thinking, but may turn into seemingly realistic concepts with manageable risk due to a comprehensive detail level and perhaps smart well-known solutions from other systems. To use a metaphor, many individuals gathered in small radical innovations groups spread around, each one with their own special character, will nourish the company's upper levels with ideas similarly to how a tree drains the soil for water and nutrition through an immense number of tiny hair-like threads, each one so small compared to the totality that the word insignificance comes to mind. Like water from these tiny roots join and bring life necessities special for each particular location, ideas will join, strengthen, be challenged, grow, breed and make up a totality far stronger than ideation without interaction (see Figure 22).

Figure 22   Illustration of the roots of a tree. In a similar way as a tree drains moisture from a large area in the soil, innovative ideas can be gathered from all corners of the company (every root branch) to be organized and systematized in strategy (the trunk) to make up optionality in the form of several future scenarios. The more widespread the roots, the more nutrition the tree gets and the more solid it stands.

What you are creating can be seen somewhat as a second organizational structure active only for a few hours a week, fortnight, month or whatever you choose. The nodes (those individuals a part of the radical group structure) restructure organizationally at their given time and establish a totally different configuration optimized for producing products of a different nature (each group may have their own time). A totally flat structure, where mixing knowledge bases and insights is the rule and methodically searching the unknown is key. Then, as quickly as the restructuring occurred, it vanishes as the company's organizational structure re-establishes just a few hours later when radical innovation time is over. Only new-borne concepts in sketch form and the impatient desire to test and further improve them deep in a number of minds that are spread out remain as prove of the activity. Organizationally it may be considered *virtual* as in virtual teams, but it is indeed cheap and effective.

Open innovation can also play a role in this structure. External ideas can be an input source to the internal group work, like are discussed in *Where to find inspiration and get ideas* on page 96. Many companies use open innovation as a direct idea source. This can indeed be valuable, but they don't benefit from the last dimension where ideas join forces and make up even better ideas and eventually complete scenarios adapted to the company strategy, resources and market potential. All this internal knowledge is hard to find from an external source directly. Also, bringing externals into the process of improving single ideas and creating viable scenarios means that ownership must be shared, which may turn into complicated agreements and contracts. It may be useful to think through these things and make agreements before involving externals – but when they are there it may prove to be a powerful mix.

Ideation is not only about finding good ideas, but also about working them into viable future scenarios for your specific organization. An efficient radical innovation network can help you with both and particularly the latter.

Portfolio example

The sea current power generator

Another innovation group in the company had made some progress within the field of power generation from sea currents. They challenged our group to come up with a unit that would allow a positive bottom line on the cost balance sheet in order to take advantage of sea currents. If successful, this would match their work perfectly. Unfortunately, I cannot share their part of this journey for confidentiality reasons.

The obvious advantage with sea current power generation is the enormous amounts of energy available in our oceans in total and its low level of intermittency compared to most other significant renewable alternatives. The downside to commercial energy extraction from sea currents is their low current speed most places on our planet, which makes the energy concentration low. The speed is really important for the energy output as the power available is proportional to the speed in the third potency. Other significant challenges include fouling and, like always, Total Cost of Ownership (TCO) to make sure it balances the income.

During the initial discussions we invited an expert on sea currents. We already had an expert on renewable energy in general and offshore floating wind turbines in particular as a fixed member of the group. Both of these became really central in the discussions that followed, but quite soon we discovered that our competence on conventional offshore oil and gas facilities could become useful. Gold can be found in the intersections between different peaks of expertise (see Figure 11). Many different options were discussed, but soon we decided to look closer at deeper installations. The rationale behind this decision was that most renewable sources struggle with a positive balance sheet, and working the cost side in the energy market seems to have the most significant impact on this crucial balance. Going deeper, away from the wind and wave affected part of the sea column would positively influence maintenance. A floating wind turbine, for example, is placed where the winds are strongest. This means that it will be heavily exposed to wave loads as well, because there is a correlation between wind and waves. In addition, there could be strong sea currents in an independent direction to the wind. All these forces need to be handled by the wind turbine structure. Installing a sea current power generator deeper in the sea column, although with a distance from the bottom, would mean really stable environmental conditions (temperature, sea current, fouling, stably low levels of foreign elements like sand/dust, sea animals etc.). This would positively influence maintenance, since the structure could be engineered to relatively precise environmental conditions. The inconvenience is that the current speed has a tendency to decrease with depth – although this is far from being always the case.

In an innovation process it may be useful to start out with a concrete case and upscale afterwards (see the 10X method in Figure 13). We chose to look at a case in the Faroe Bank Channel. Here the warm sea from the south slowly flows north over the majority of the sea column. However, far down on the sea column, close to the bottom, the current shifts direction. The warm current from the south cools down in the North Sea, and as such it becomes heavier and sinks down. This effect fills the North Sea basin up from the bottom with cold water until the cold water flows over the Faroe Bank Channel and flows into the larger Atlantic Ocean. The sea current speed on the bottom at this location is approximately one meter per second and fairly constant[15], and it is a super place for a sea current power generator not too far away from major power markets.

Now, how to make, install and maintain fairly advanced machinery at such a location? We started to work on a concept with self-regulating buoyancy, similar to Argo Floats for example, which have the ability to sink, rise or stay buoyant as required. This can be done by using a flexible container, like a balloon, containing a gas, which would create lift in a floating element. The size of this "balloon" can be controlled by a compressor by evacuating the gas from the balloon and storing it in a connected fixed volume container by increasing the gas pressure in the container. The reduced balloon volume is replaced with sea water.

This will result in a relatively heavier system, which eventually will turn a positive buoyancy to negative, leading the system to start sinking.

We started out with a rim driven thruster type of generator, which would transfer the blade rotation to electric power directly, opposite to a rim driven thruster on ships that transfers electric power to blade rotation, which again pushes a boat in the desired direction (see Research Disclosure database number 663066 for more details). This would allow us to pull our generator out to location behind the service vessel, and change buoyancy on location to put the generator in place (see Figure 23).

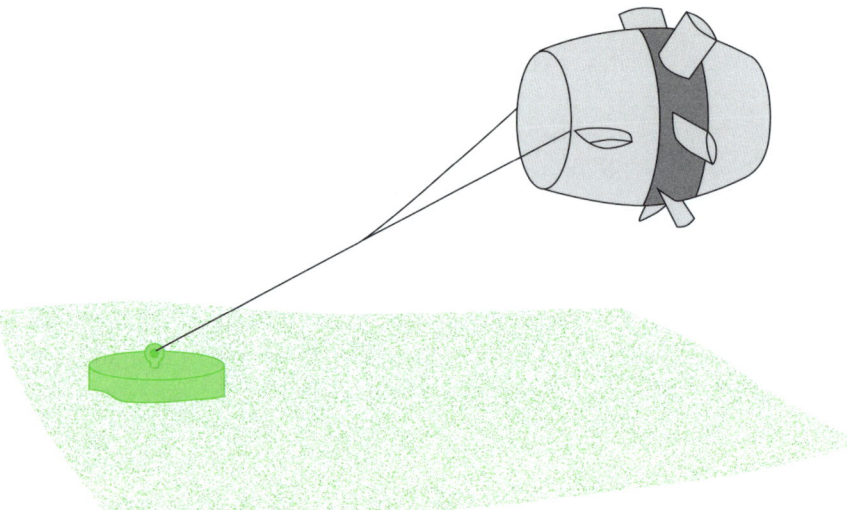

Figure 23 First version of our sea current machine.

To hold the generator firmly in place we decided to use a suction anchor as fixation to the bottom and mooring between the anchor and the generator. A suction anchor can be compared to an upside-down bucket on the seabed where a small pump evacuates the sea water inside the bucket. This will create a vacuum like effect inside the bucket which will pull the structure into the sediments on the seabed. The anchoring capacity of a suction anchor is tremendously high. This concept has been applied in the oil and gas sector for decades for different applications like anchors. Another clear advantage with such an anchor is that it can be remotely installed from sea surface. The idea was to send out a vessel with anchor, mooring including electric cables as well as generator. The latter could be placed either on deck or floating behind. The connection point to the preinstalled electric network has also a self-regulating buoyancy plug which can be called via the electric network to come to the surface. Here this plug can be connected to the generator via the anchor and the mooring. Now the suction anchor is lowered into the sea, placed on the seabed, evacuated and sucked into place. At this point the anchor is in place and the generator is floating on the sea surface. The self-regulating buoyancy system in the generator is activated and the generator slowly sinks into place floating a desired distance above the seabed. Remote flow measurement systems, like the Lidar system, can measure the best flow conditions and direct the generator into position for the highest possible power generation at all times.

Due to generally slow sea currents, other places on earth than the Faroe Bank Channel where the current is economically viable are sparse. To increase profitable operating space across our planet, we choose to look for designs that would increase the speed through our tunnel. First attempt was the venturi concept (see publication). We made a simple axi-symmetric CFD (Computed Fluid Dynamics) analyses on the venture design and discovered that we could almost double the speed through the tunnel compared to the ambient current velocity. This doubling was, however, achievable with an empty tunnel without turbine and generator in place.

One of the issues we needed to come around was how to keep the generator housing steady and the rotor blades rotating. A simple mooring cable would not be able to transfer torque and would spin until failure. Two or more mooring strings would help, but in order to save cost and maintain flexibility to move the generator both vertically and horizontally in the hunt for stronger local currents or to escape possible floating elements with damage potential, we wanted to avoid a second set of anchor and mooring. We decided to go for static wings outside the generator housing with adjustable angle to the current direction in order to adjust the counter torque to perfectly balance the torque generated by the rotor.

When trying this concept on experts on shipping, we soon learned that we had to reconsider the static blades on the housing. The complexity of the regulation system would be high and the manufacturing cost of hardware high too. We reworked this element and came to the conclusion that two generators next to each other, rotating the opposite way, would balance the system out quite well. There was still a need for regulating the blades or wings on the housing, but they would have far less work keeping the structure producing power steadily.

Figure 24   Second twin turbine design with suction anchor and mooring. (Source: Inventas)

We also needed to work with the flow through the tunnel. Generating speed over the blades is vital to maximize the amount of power possible of generating. One of the reasons to choose a rim driven thruster was that the tunnel could be designed to create the venturi effect, which increases the speed through while lowering the pressure through the venture shape. We decided to make a numerical study of the flow through our generator tunnel on the open market outside our company. The study indicated that the venturi principle would give us an effect, but another design would boost the speed through our tunnel even more. A tunnel where the exit diameter is substantially larger than the inlet diameter would have a positive effect on our power generation. The diverging cross section through the tunnel would decrease the speed through the tunnel as the cross-section area increases, while the speed near the surface on the outside will quite oppositely increase the near surface water speed. With the housing angle under a certain angle, the two flows will meet at the rear face of the turbine. The fast outer flow will pull the flow through the tunnel along, which again will increase the flow through the channel. In this study we also added a resistance in the tunnel simulating the blades. We discovered that the new design actually maintained a doubling of the speed through our turbine even after adding a resistance equivalent to the power extraction turbine itself. Until now the speed had been measured at the center line.

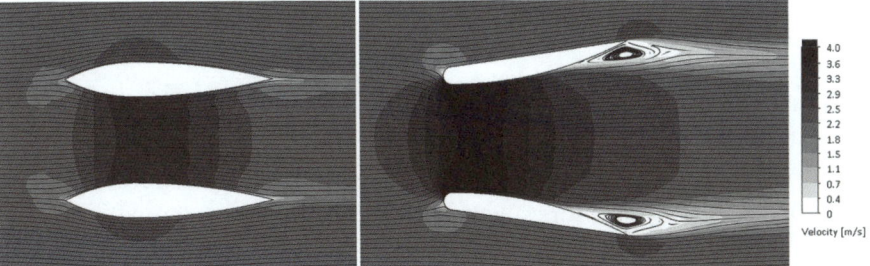

Figure 25 Numerical study indicating the difference between two duct designs, where current speed increases from light grey to black. White is the housing cross section and flow direction is from left to right. (Source: Inventas)

> Doubling the speed through the tunnel would give a significant energy increase compared to using the ambient speed directly. But most places this would still not be enough to give significant energy outputs due to slow currents. We decided to try a new design enforcing the diverging tunnel effect. The idea was to make the exit wavy in order to increase the total area at which the outer higher velocity water pulls slower water along through the tunnel, making this pull effect stronger. The hope was that this effect would be stronger than the increased friction a larger housing surface would bring. Simulations showed however, that these two effects were more or less the same and had little effect on the speed through the tunnel. In fact, there was a slight decrease, which led us to leave this design change option, which after all would increase the manufacturing cost and complexity significantly.
>
> At the moment of writing, this project is still ongoing and is receiving attention from different parts of the company. It was born as two radical groups joined forces and pursued something as ambitious as low intermittency green energy.

Build a direct communication channel to the leadership

But how to pass all the gateways from the root tip in Figure 22 as a naked idea on the floor all the way to the trunk, which is top leadership whose role is to lead the way by maintaining or changing direction?

Ambidexterity

To answer this, we have to look at the basic mechanisms in play. The very nature of radical innovation is to challenge present direction. Only the company leadership, or more specifically the CEO, has the mandate to actually change company direction (see *Radical innovation on different levels in the company* on page 123 for radical solutions that do not challenge the company direction). In fact, not only is this in the CEO's mandate, it is his/her main task to lead the way and turn when necessary, preferably *before* it is screamingly necessary. A central question is then, how prepared does the project have to be before the company leadership can spend time on this? For mainstream projects, typically in process improvement, cost saving, increased productivity, enhanced quality type of projects, all of which normally are referred to as incremental, quality assurance follows the line to the top. The likelihood is that these projects improve for every gateway they pass since the gate keeper is in this position because he/she knows a lot about the present solution, he/she feels the pressure to improve the situation, he/she has the ability to imagine the effect of the change, and he/she can make sound prioritizations between this and all other relevant improvement proposals on the table due to insight into the project portfolio, budgets, risk, cost and predicted effects. In addition, he/she will add new knowledge to an already solid personal knowledge base on the subject and as such strengthen his/her leading position on the field. Nor is it a disadvantage that this type of improvement probably is a well-established subject in appraisal talks. Everything is in place for a valuable incremental proposal *to improve and mature during the climbing process up the organization*. For all these reasons, many of the decisions associated to this type of "straightforward" incremental improvements normally do not need sanctioning from the top, and can be decided on lower levels.

Radical concepts struggle more climbing upwards through gateways on its way to the top. Middle management and experts get into awkward positions facing radical proposals. One clear reason is the discrepancy between their knowledge base and what is required. Radical means ploughing new ground. As a consequence, the ability for both middle management (Note: not upper leadership) and experts of the existing solution to make sound considerations about feasibility, risk levels, time to market and future revenues related to radical proposals is very limited. In fact, they are inclined to take a negative attitude since the possible success of the radical concept will make their expertise and experience base obsolete. And who wants to play themselves out of the game? The chance is that the concept will meet resistance, consciously or perhaps more subconsciously. This is fortified by the fear of the unknown and the not-invented-here syndrome. For management a new-born radical concept is surely not on the deliverable list for the year. Neither do they know enough about the overall strategy to be able to judge whether to place the project inside or outside the development direction of the company. Often there are limited benefits for a gate keeper (middle management or discipline expert) to approve a wild concept, while there can certainly be negative consequences in the case of failure. This makes a *negative* answer safer than a *positive*. After all, if you stop a project, you are almost sure to be right; it will not succeed if no attempt is made – if you say yes it may still fail.

All of this makes experts and middle management inclined to prefer lower risk incremental suggestions rather than higher risk radical proposals. In practical terms management and experts can function as a filter for radical concepts. Assuming that the company's upper leadership, whose main role is to lead by pointing out the company's direction, would like as broad a vision of the possible future scenarios as possible to base any directional choice on, the company leadership would appreciate a constant flow of radical proposals. When reporting these radical concepts through the hierarchy in the same way as more standard incremental efforts, going the line way to the top, they stand the chance of being filtered away or changed into more subtle sub-optimal direction alterations *before* they reach intended destination at the top. This is why companies adapt *ambidextrous leadership* when evaluating developments [5-9]; ambidextrous literally means "two handed", which in this context refers to two different handling and approval routes for standard incremental ideas on one hand and more radical ideas on the other (see the two routes summed up in Figure 27). The incremental goes the line way and is prioritized through net present value considerations. Radical ideas jump the management level and are sanctioned on the upper leadership level based more on an overall consideration of the total portfolio making up the new direction. These ideas can by all means get feedback from middle management and experts on the way, but these are considered additional information and not go/no-go decisions.

Let us look at a metaphor meant to illustrate the difference between incremental and radical innovation in this context, and why the two need to be considered differently. Let us imagine that our value creation is a cash machine resting on different foundations (see Figure 26)

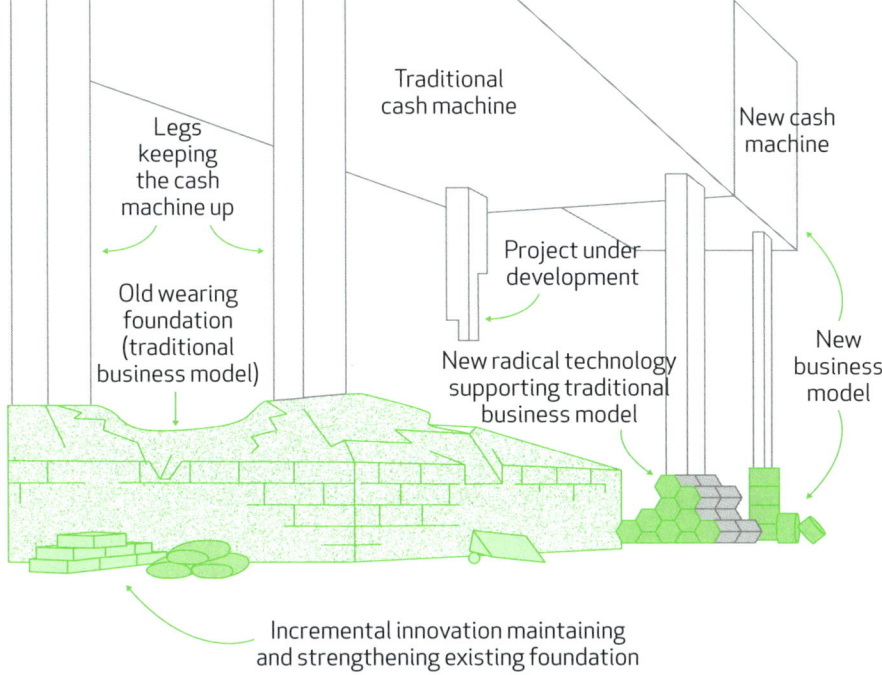

Figure 26 Metaphor: A company is a cash machine resting its legs on different foundations. The foundations are exposed to weathering and erosion and need maintenance and even strengthening to support growing (incremental innovation). However, to advance requires more legs to rest on to inherently increase the balance and stability. New legs and new foundations on new soil are radical, disruptive innovation. These foundations can be built with totally different building blocks.

Considering our dynamic world where new products come and go, where fashion, habits, competition and consumer psychology can turn a successful product into history in a short while, our cash machine is more stable with several preferably solid foundations to rest on. Our foundations erode over time since static things are in contradiction to our dynamic world. New products affect the market of the old, and the age necessary to qualify as old is constantly shrinking. Incremental innovation in this metaphor is maintenance of these traditional foundations to counterwork erosion and perhaps even strengthen them. Practically this means improving the products by for example quality improvement, new design, reduced price and so on.

 Those who do not advance recede.

New foundations represent radically different value chains that are detached in the sense that they do not build on the competence and experience of the old product (or business model). In the illustrations these foundations are independently placed in a separate location than the traditional foundation and built with different bricks (= knowledge).

In an ambidextrous setting, the strategy department designs these foundations, making sure that the foundations added together can support the cash machine (= bring net value to the company). In the design phase, they also make sure that the foundation is complete with all necessary solutions (= bricks) in the sense that there are no holes making the foundation too weak. Not all bricks need to be great new solutions individually, but can still represent an important part to build a viable new foundation, which as a whole makes a positive contribution. From the S-curves (see Figure 5) we know that even in great new solutions, the central new bricks that will carry much of the weight in the new foundation will initially come out less efficient than the matured solutions in the traditional foundation when directly compared. The difference is that the future growth potential is huge while the traditional foundation in the mature phase takes a lot of effort even for a slight growth.

In a setting where no ambidexterity exists, the tendency is that "funny looking" bricks for the new foundation will be judged individually by the maintenance crew of the traditional foundation. From their perspective with traditional bricks making up the traditional foundation, how can they objectively evaluate how suitable the newly shaped bricks can be in a different unknown context? Or said differently, middle management and experts who spend their day improving elements in the present/traditional value chain, will look at new radical solutions out of context and are therefore not in a position to judge whether they pass or not. Adding a strong focus on cost consciousness on top of this, it is clear that this system is a fine-meshed filter for new radical ideas, and a system for lost opportunities rather than the preferable opposite.

Note also that the traditional foundation is wider and more massive than the newer foundation(s). This is meant to illustrate that the traditional value chain is composed of a portfolio of products, processes, procedures and/or services including supporting offers. The newer value chain starts on a narrower base with for example one product, which can over time expand and take on "weight" distributed over more than single bricks.

Also, there comes a point beyond which no maintenance can make a positive contribution to the old foundation of the cash machine. For example, no matter how efficient your foundation maintenance crew (= development department) is, they will not manage to increase the value creation of for example kerosene lamps (paraffin lamps). They are simply outdated.

In practice, ambidextrous leadership can be executed by handling incremental and radical projects in different processes, in different organizational units or even in separate subsidiaries/companies on a later stage.

Radical innovation on different levels in the company

The previous section discussed ambidexterity in an innovation context, which essentially suggests handling incremental innovation through the line, while radical innovation is directed to top leadership level where the company's future direction is being constantly evaluated. But does this mean that all radical innovation has to go via top executives? Not really. Radical solutions with a radical effect on the company should indeed be sanctioned at top level, since they are responsible for the company's direction. Incremental innovation with an incremental effect can go the line way since this supports the already decided direction and gets the best support where the experts are organized. But all innovation is not that black and white. The shades of grey in this context are incremental solutions with a radical effect for the company and radical solutions with an incremental effect. Let's look at some examples.

Incremental solutions with a radical effect could be a plane manufacturer's effort to save cost and weight by reducing dimensions on components to a minimum. If they go too far and a vital part fails during service, the plane might fall down and cause a catastrophe, which definitely would have a radical effect on the company. A company's protection against this type of surprises are effects like strict qualification procedures, comprehensive test programs, safety margins and so on.

Radical solutions with an incremental effect could be to exchange all the classic light bulbs with LEDs in a cost saving project in order to save both power and maintenance. The LED solution is indeed a radical solution compared to classic resistance lighting considering the definition of radical solutions (see More about on page 17), but the effect of replacing these classic light sources with LED's will have an incremental effect on cost saving in most companies. In this case the maintenance group responsible for lighting might clear this point with their manager, who would consider this an incremental change and would not hesitate to make the decision within his/her responsibility frame.

In the LED light case, the radical solution does obviously not need to pass by the executive level for a decision, even if LED can be argued radical compared to the present lighting. The reason is that it will not have any effect on the company's direction. Quite on the contrary it will support the direction the upper leadership already have decided, delegated downwards and materialized in a cost saving project on execution level. Therefore, the LED solution needs to pass by the project manager of the cost saving project and sanctioned there since it is within the scope of his/her project. The same principle applies for other radical solutions which do not lead to a new direction for the company as a whole. All these radical solutions may be considered radical by nature many levels upwards, but common to them all is that they will meet a level at which the suggestion is to be considered incremental since it supports and not challenges the present company direction at this level. This is the level at which the radical suggestion should be sanctioned. Otherwise the same ambidexterity applies for these grey-shaded radical solutions as the black-and-white radical solutions with an effect on the company direction; incremental and radical ideas are treated differently in separate channels.

Reporting route not a one-way street
An important part of strategy work is to map out possible company directions by establishing viable future scenarios composed of clear, visual radical concepts. These are best worked out where the hands-on core competence exists – in the intersections of everyday work. Ideally, however, this is not a one-way street from the floor where day-to-day work tasks are performed and up to the top. As mentioned before, making the creative process into a systematic process starts with a business need – this need should be communicated top down to assure that creative efforts are relevant for the company. Well, new need proposals can come from anywhere, but they have to pass by strategy at the leadership level, be organized and sanctioned as a prioritized business need.

However, this type of dialogue between the leadership and the radical innovation groups should not stop with a stated business or customer need. In the spirit of Erik Ries' Lean Startup theory, radical concepts communicated back to the top (as a result of a received need or meaningful direction for sought solutions) should be considered proposals, or in Lean Startup terms, minimum viable products (MVP's). In this context, the leadership is the customer, from whom the radical innovation groups get feedback on their efforts as useful guidance on further development. The overview stays at the strategy level, where feedback can go to individual groups, but also bringing particularly interesting groups with similar or complementing proposals together to further enhance the position in chosen directions. Although these groups will get insight into their contribution to the overall strategy, it remains only a part of the totality, a totality that stays at the top level. Strategic work is after all stock market sensitive, so distribution should be limited.

At this point it is worth commenting on the similarities and differences between the *Future Scenarios* argued for in this book and the more well-known *Scenario Planning* also called Scenario Thinking/Analysis that one of Equinor's competitors is particularly known to practice. Both these processes look into the future and both use creativity to foresee what might happen. However, the Scenario Planning tool is often used to train key personnel to be prepared for what may be inflicted upon them from their surroundings by picking out different scenarios and plan actions to handle or counteract the imaginary situation. Creativity is used to respond to the made-up scenarios presented. As an example a scenario could be, "in five years energy is free – how do we as an energy company meet this change?" Participants would have to propose how the company should react to this scenario, to limit damage and pursue opportunities in a holistic perspective. Viable Future Scenarios in this book does not start with extreme future situations imposed on us by our surroundings, but present needs and contemporary realistic trends. Creativity is put into how the company could meet these needs in a different way than our current value creation would react. A goal is to make several possible options that are attractive future opportunities, all of which could compete with the current value creation. To be attractive the future scenario needs to take external factors into account, but the future scenario is proactively challenging the future. In this case the end result is what matters, while in the Scenario Planning method, the process is as important as the final result, since the training is meant to create participants prepared for a range of future situations. Scenario Planning, being a response to external changes, is more reactive in nature, although the very reason for training is to prepare the company for such scenarios and allow a more proactive response. Another difference is at which level the creativity takes place in the company. While Scenario Planning often takes place at executive levels, Viable Future Scenarios are worked out by groups composed of individuals who are chosen based on a set of criteria, within which company level is not represented. Individuals tend to come from throughout the organization and would therefore normally have a higher number of representatives from lower organizational levels simply since they out-number executives.

Future Scenarios and Scenario Planning are two scenario-based techniques with clear similarities but also significant differences.

Evaluating radical innovation projects

To build an effective radical innovation network with strategy pulling all the strings as is discussed above, it is key to know how to evaluate early phase radical concepts including how this stands out from evaluating incremental improvement projects. This theory is based on the assumption that all radical ideas change during maturation – and they really do. Incremental ideas, on the other hand, are about smaller steps in the same direction. If they should change dramatically, you could argue they wouldn't be incremental anymore. All radical ideas change during the course of time. However, to the extent one can generalize, the core intent often stays the same. Therefore, the core should be emphasized in early phase concept evaluation more than the nitty-gritty details, which are with a high probability going to change anyway. The core intention relates to the strategic direction and is a leadership matter, while the details that will "carry" or "deliver" the core intention, are more an engineering task.

To exemplify the core theory with the horse and tractor example: the core intention may have been to introduce an Otto engine as a more unlimited and flexible power source anywhere on the farm where the reliability was linked to the supply of fuel and not the wellbeing of livestock. This intention should be in the center of an evaluation discussion, and not the more peripheral parts like the number of wheels, belts around the wheels or not, engine in the front or back, which standard to choose on the power outlet connection, etc. These things will most likely change many times over the first few years anyway, and should not by themselves stand in the way of the main intention.

Early stage radical innovation is more searching an area, rather than promoting a specific idea. If you are on the evaluation side, you may want to consider a radical concept in this way – as a part of an ongoing search where you need to make sure that the basic objective is within scope, and the rest is up for discussion.

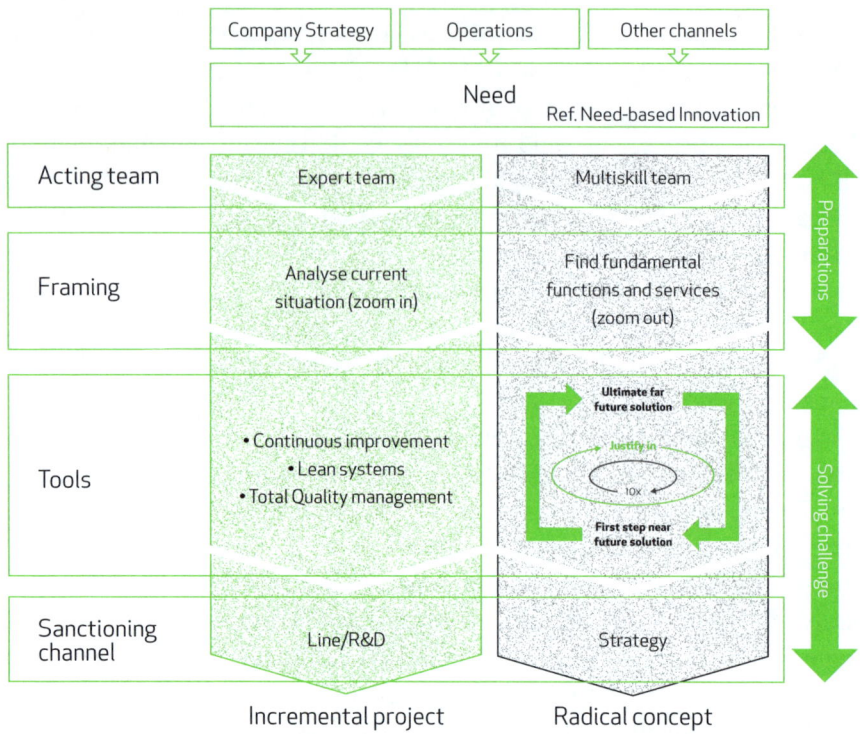

Figure 27 Illustration of innovation ambidexterity: how the processes and the process input are different when an incremental project (green column) versus a radical concept (gray column) are harvested from an established need.

Radical innovation as workshops for non-skilled

So far, we have been discussing how to build up an organizational structure where radical innovation is systematically created on regular basis. This structure is founded on individual skills making up group skills built over time, applying methods to create viable ideas following dedicated routes for idea maturation. The regular participants are the backbone of this structure who maintain and develop the habit of looking at challenges from a different perspective, temporarily lowering the guard for risk and uncertainty while searching the unknown. Innovation skills and experience are obviously important in creating valuable results, but can we also create value using participants without skills associated to radical ideation and innovation more in an occasional task force or workshop type of setting?

Single workshops built on the same philosophy can also indeed be effective without participants already skilled on radical innovation. I have facilitated numerous workshops like this in Equinor with great results. The system is relatively simple. Invite a multiskill group, since multiskills are essential for the creation of radical solutions (see *Core group members* on page 46). A unique possibility to pave the way for potential solutions in the future is inviting key stakeholders and individuals who may influence the project as it goes forward. This is particularly the case for those you expect may cause trouble later in the project simply since early involvement in the creation has a positive effect. It is generally also considered positive that stakeholders see that solutions come as a result of a thorough and logical method involving representatives from all thinkable view angles.

The multiskill element can also be an effective way to get around challenges associated to limited information flow in a company (often referred to as "silo work") simply by involving competence in adjacent disciplines and others with direct or indirect interfaces to the subject of the workshop. They help you mature your mandate, but they could also bring the knowledge of your plans back to their own camp where the likelihood of alignment between plans and ultimately actions increase. This will be elaborated on under *Radical innovation to assure agility in project-based work* on page 134.

A workshop is typically divided into three main stages:

1. Formulate the basic challenge (which question to ask)
2. How does the extreme solution look (often the far future solution)
3. Roadmap – how to get to the extreme solution.

The reasons for these simple steps are the same as those we have touched upon earlier in this book.

Stage 1: Formulate the basic challenge

Spending some time to formulate the basic challenge together has several important objectives (see also More about page 72). First and foremost, it is important for everyone in the workshop to have the same challenge clear in mind as they move into the creative part of the workshop and start to interact. Since the objective is to get radical results, it is important for the facilitator to make sure that the challenge addresses the *fundamental* company (or customer) need in order to make room for solutions of a different nature (see *Work method for radical innovation* on page 66 for more on fundamental needs). Secondly, formulating a common challenge owned by the company or a customer has a tremendous alignment effect. This disarms potential conflicts between different power centers such as departments or knowledge hubs or disciplines, which may occur in settings where different human environments are mixed to realize real multiskill. The "need owner" must be chosen as being high enough for everyone present to feel ownership. For example, when I have participants from large parts of the company, my need-statement is anchored in the company ("Equinor needs…"), in order for everyone present to feel the need is relevant to them. Next to being important for the rest of the workshop, such a need formulation built by participants from all relevant parts of the challenge has a value in itself. As such it is valuable to spend time developing the need together.

In addition to the need statement, I recommend listing the most important solution neutral qualities a solution should meet. These will serve as more or less a conscious evaluation criterion throughout the workshop against which the participants can assess potential solutions. Examples of such qualities could be low cost, efficiency, environmentally friendly, new level of user experience, simple man/machine interface, fully automated etc.

However, sometimes there is not enough time to do a full workshop. In these cases, I have cut down on this first stage – the need or challenge statement. Under such circumstances I have engaged selected key players to formulate a need statement to the best of their ability before the workshop. Then I have taken that need statement and blackened out a couple of key words and presented this to all participants in the beginning of the workshop, challenging them to suggest which words I have temporarily removed. They start by reflecting on the challenge individually (which will be explained more in detail below) perhaps writing down these suggestions for example on post-it notes. Then I ask everyone to come up with suggestions. This allows a quality check of the need statement, but more importantly, it forces everyone present to be critical to the need statement which will bring it straight into the center of attention for the rest of the day. Although this quick and often more entertaining way to distribute the need statement may update and improve the proposed statement, it will probably not change it totally. This again means that saving time is achieved at the expense of a challenge or need statement built from scratch by the entire group.

Stage 2: Develop the extreme solution

Now that all participants know which basic need to address and which challenge to attack, it is time to look for solutions. For small safe (incremental) steps forward, you may want to look critically at present solutions (if they exist) and from there search for an improvement potential. However, if you look for larger steps and more radical solutions, you would do better by first looking away from the present solutions and go extreme. Extreme in this context is going further than the solution you are looking for. Time is a classic extreme scale. If you are looking for a solution three years down the road, you would in this stage (No. 2) typically look much further into the future – say ten or even fifteen years. If you are looking for a cost reduction of 20%, going extreme could be to find out how a 50% cost reduction solution would look. The same principle can be applied on other properties of the solution sought, like size, efficiency (performance), durability, simplification, user experience and so on.

The idea is that we start the creative process by looking at an overall direction before we take the first step. The far future solution would give us that direction. This also moves our mental anchor away from the present solution and into the future, which in itself makes us take longer steps (see more on this subject in *Radical innovation not only for tomorrow but also today* on page 153). In addition, the effect of looking further into the future than your delivery commitment, offers participants to be more relaxed about minor practical challenges and presently perceived obstacles, and dive further into the creative bonanza. This is when participants laugh, share, build, listen, think, talk and laugh even more.

Stage 3: Make a roadmap

When the extreme solutions are shining as bright guiding stars, the preparation phase is over and it is time to start creating tangible value. The guiding star shows direction and even roughly a possible future state, on which the mental anchor is now firmly fixed. Evaluating this state against the state of today results in a gap analysis. Stage No. 3 is about making that gap analysis and planning how to best close the gap. The participants try to list the necessary activities, consider how comprehensive each task is, how tasks interact to offer steady progress and last but not least the value they offer both independently and as a part of the totality. For radical innovation endorsement is not only a question about demonstrating high value post implementation, but to prove positive value in key building blocks all the way from start to finish. That is not to say that all tasks have to offer value all the time. The puzzle is to plan activities in a sequence that steadily develop the final solution while offering financial returns regularly all the way to the end where the real price awaits. However, it is also about assuring that those beneficial activities pave the way for those indispensable activities that in themselves do not offer any value creation before final implementation. Such planning is quite demanding and takes more creativity than one might think.

Energizing and aligning everyone through all stages

So far, the workshop doesn't stand out significantly from work in the regular radical innovation groups. However, to maximize the knowledge distribution by assuring contributions from all participants, also including those not used to creative processes like these, certain measures may prove useful through each of the three workshop stages described above.

Each stage starts with a few minutes, perhaps three to five, of individual reflection. The aim is that each participant gets the opportunity, undisturbed and alone, to "empty" the brain for proposals on the specific task given by the need statement. Individual reflection normally results in a high number of immature ideas. I normally ask the participants to note their ideas on post-it notes, requesting one idea per note in order to facilitate sorting at a later stage.

Now that a high quantity with more or less relevant ideas are generated, it is time to join predefined groups carefully composed based on multiskill. An optimal group size is three to five persons. Larger groups have a tendency to become inefficient in that fewer people actively talk and more people passively listen at any time, considering the workshop as a whole. It also seems like about five people is a tipping point beyond which many people hesitate to share "out of the box" ideas. The task now is to share and sort all ideas followed by a qualitative group judgement of the contributions in order to choose which ideas to keep working on in the following and include in the groups prototype. Here it is worth commenting a positive side effect of having ideas noted on paper from the individual reflection. Without notes you run the risk that the most outgoing persons would keep talking at the expense of more reserved people. With notes to categorize, the chance is that everyone is heard and all ideas in the group are candidates for the prototype. The best ideas are now joined into a total solution suggestion, which can be seen as a hand-drawn solution prototype. The solution prototype looks very different for the different stages described above. The prototype of Stage 1, the basic challenge, is normally a written need statement containing all the important aspects of the sought solution, in order to guide the rest of the work. A workshop run by a car manufacturer could write the basic challenge statement of their new economy vehicle in this way:

The "company" needs to extend the model portfolio with a new bestselling vehicle with a return balance above "XX" that is
- Appealing to women between 18 and 30 years of age
- World leading in safety in its class
- Sold at a competitive price below the average cost in its class
- Emitting zero CO_2 in use

...and so on.

The prototype of Stage 2, the extreme solution, is usually a busy hand-drawn sketch on a large poster type paper of the solution with comments, numbers and simple estimations connected to drawing details with simple arrows and perhaps explanatory boxes describing different associated processes, all of which are meant to explain the group's ideas to the rest of the workshop participants fast and effectively. The prototype of Stage 3, the roadmap, is normally a Gantt type diagram with a list of activities associated with an arrow in the time scale, or simply a timeline over which a number of the post-it notes from the previous stage plus a few new ones are scattered. No matter which of these two the group chooses to apply, the important part is to be able to effectively communicate the group's ideas to the other teams during the last part of every stage, which takes place in plenum.

The last part of each stage is prototype sharing with everyone present and preferably actively participating in discussions. The groups, or rather chosen representatives from each group, present the group's prototypes one after the other. As soon as the second prototype is shared, the facilitator starts to compare the prototypes by highlighting similarities, but in particular discuss significant differences with everyone in order to debate which of the two suits the purpose best, not ruling out that both can be viable parts of the end result. It is indeed amazing how such a process taps into many people's minds and boils a large amount of information down to the key areas of conflicts and potential. It is also worth noting that the process anonymizes the idea proposer through the group work, so that any idea of the sort that one would hesitate to personally share in larger crowds, will in this process be associated with a group and no longer a person. This raises the social safety factor and I would say also the creative potential.

Radical innovation to assure agility in project-based work

Next to establishing radical innovation groups as a part of daily routines in the company and organizing occasional creative workshops, the same principles can with advantage be used in project-based work where the project needs to deliver previously unknown solutions and as such requires innovation. To elaborate using the jungle metaphor from *Shepherd leadership and framing the search* on page 85, the route of the project goes through unknown terrain, which means pioneering is needed to support the procession. Pioneering is the agile, multiskilled group discovering new potential solutions and the procession is more the traditional fixed hierarchical structure with defined work tasks to deliver those plans. Pioneering and procession are terms used in the explanation below.

The main intention is to offer fairly large projects a method to provide agility, creativity, integrated solutions and the ability to stretch further into the future. The method splits the planning part from the hands-on work to deliver the plans. It creates a project structure, which on one hand allows agile planning assuring that all aspects of the task at hand are available simultaneously offering continuous learning and adjustment throughout the planning phase, while on the other hand assures a more structured progress according to the plan for effective advancement.

Applying the proposed method, the tendency is that:

- Plans are updated frequently with a cross discipline consensus which allows the project to iterate faster towards a solution generally accepted to be optimal throughout the project, all within the frames of the project.
- The project is likely to stretch further in the desired direction.
- All relevant parties are involved in forming the entire solution and contribute beyond each one's specific discipline or responsibility area, which raises quality within and across disciplines, which again facilitates implementation, integration and/or hand over.
- Involvement and an alignment effect smooth out pretensions and initial disagreements.
- Information distribution and general awareness improve as a secondary effect of involvement, which reduces the need for non-productive formal reporting.
  - This again allows every contributor to appreciate not only the isolated effect of their own contributions, but also the effects on the overall picture.

The challenge to make an optimal overall delivery with integrated sub-solutions based on synergies over responsibility interfaces increases with the size of the project. The reason is that larger projects are divided into responsible sub-projects. Introvert focus also often comes with this responsibility, which makes optimization work and cooperation across sub-projects very challenging and therefore also limited. This is often referred to as "working in silos" resulting in a sub-optimal overall delivery, which therefore is undesirable.

To overcome the silo effect and move from sub-optimization to project excellence, the current method divides pioneering (planning and innovation) and procession work (execution of the plans). The pioneer work is short sessions from time-to-time based on radical innovation principles where current plans are evaluated against actual progress and new plans are made based on cooperation across disciplines with the creative input from all parts of the project and even beyond. The pioneering work is similar to the workshops described in the previous section (see *Radical innovation as workshops for non-skilled* on page 128). This represents a small portion of the total time available, probably less than five percent. The procession work is the daily work between the pioneering sessions to deliver on the actions decided during planning, which then represent the rest of the time (probably more than 95%). These two principally different work modes will be elaborated in the next two sections.

"Pioneering" to imagine, stretch, plan and inform

The pioneer work would typically be relatively large workshops where representatives from all parts of the project as well as other relevant resources are represented. Other relevant resources could be representatives:

- possessing necessary knowledge and experience (not held within the project)
- of owners, steering committee members and other stakeholders
- from customers and users
- from a relevant public office
- from any relevant entity expected to cause problems (involvement in this process has an aligning effect).

The purpose is to organize workshops according to the radical innovation principles elaborated in this book (for example the right side of Figure 27) and specifically those described in *Radical innovation as workshops for non- skilled* on page 128, in order to:

1. define the challenge by asking the right questions
2. seek what is possible by looking too far into the future applying "justify in"
3. making a value proposition by
   a. stretching to achieve the best proposed solution within the present frames by applying "justify out" on the future solution until a feasible solution within the current time frame is found
   b. dividing the proposed solution into logic actionable sub-systems according to the available disciplines (e.g. plumbers are best doing plumbing work)
4. reorganize into procession configuration and execute (see the following section *"Procession" to effectuate the plans* on page 143)

Figure 28 below is an illustration of the different building blocks in the project planning work.

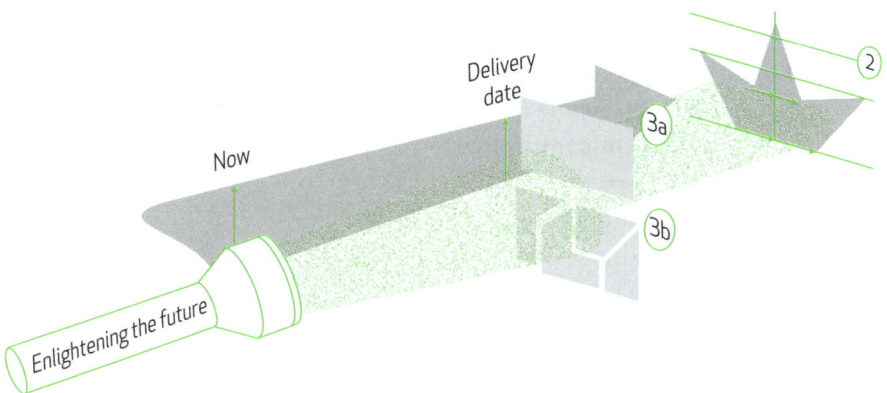

Figure 28 Illustration of project planning where, after Step 1 defining the challenge, Step 2 is looking too far into the future to find what is possible, Step 3a is extracting the solution to be realized from Step 2, and Step 3b is dividing the solution into actionable work-packages.

All workshops start by framing the innovative challenge for that specific workshop. Everyone participates in defining and articulating the challenge at hand. Most will have an idea about what the challenge is, nevertheless a common statement should be written. The main intention is that everyone upfront must have the same clear understanding of the innovative job to be done – the overall purpose of the workshop. This will obviously make it easier for the participants to effectively reach common solutions, but also, perhaps less obviously, this exercise also has a tendency to align the participants. Focusing on what the project owner or the clients need, takes the focus away from internal conflicts. Such conflicts can be of the type; "their sub-project always takes short cuts which gives us ten times more work than what they saved" or "our competence seems less valuable than theirs because whenever there is a conflict, we end up doing what they say". This alignment effect is the reason why it could be useful to invite representatives from entities that may cause problems at a later stage in the project. *Early involvement, commonly defining the real need from everyone's perspective and searching for solutions in the long-term perspective have the amazing effect of smoothing out initial differences.*

When the frames of the challenge are clear to everyone, the next task in the workshop is to start developing an imaginary far future solution to assure a long-term perspective in order to prepare the ground for the real solution to be developed (see Step 2 in Figure 28). This step applies *justify in* (see *Implement efficient innovation work methods that yield radical results* on page 58). The intention of this step is to create a distance to the present solutions, enhance creativity by stretching everyone's minds and filling the room with unconstrained innovative thoughts. In a far future solution, which will undoubtedly never be realized, the tendency is that the participants reduce their focus on problems and limitations while increasing the focus on existing possibilities. The far future solution should absolutely be a far stretch, but not far to the extent that the result doesn't make sense as a guiding star for the real solution.

Next, after establishing a vision about how our challenge might look in the far future, the workshop participants define the real solution that the project is dedicated to materializing and delivering (see Step 3a in Figure 28).

This task can follow the far future solution in the same workshop or be done in a dedicated workshop later (in which case the frame of the challenge needs to be revisited). This step applies *justify out* to the far future solution. In practical terms, this means that the participants need to justify why they would like to take elements out of the far future solution. Since, inherently the far future solution contains elements not possible at present, it should obviously not be too difficult to argue about their removal. These solutions will have to be replaced with feasible ones. Taking away something too innovative within the available time frame takes away some of the hesitation of adding something rather innovative on the achievable side of the feasibility limit. The fact that you need to argue about getting things removed from the far future solution adds to the stretch tendency in that where there are less valid arguments for removal, the deliverable solution may continue to contain these "far future" elements.

When the real deliverable solution is established, a concept is borne. Depending on the project size it might be useful to divide the solution into sub-projects with dedicated responsibilities in order to create a project structure more suitable for execution (see Step 3b in Figure 28). With such a division the chance is that the sub-projects will start to live their own separate lives, at least to a certain extent, at the expense of elegant integrated solutions in the work to follow. This leads to sub-optimization, which represents a real threat to an optimized total solution. To overcome this effect, the same workshop-based planning can also be continued with advantage in further planning of the sub-projects. Each sub-project takes the lead to organize similar types of innovative workshops as described above in order to make plans for their respective sub-project involving representatives *from all sub-projects*, and even beyond if necessary (see Figure 29). The purpose is to establish an executable plan for the organizing sub-project with input from the other sub-projects with particular focus on interfaces, dependencies, limitations, particularly new possibilities and possible synergies, all in order to minimize sub-optimization and maximize integration.

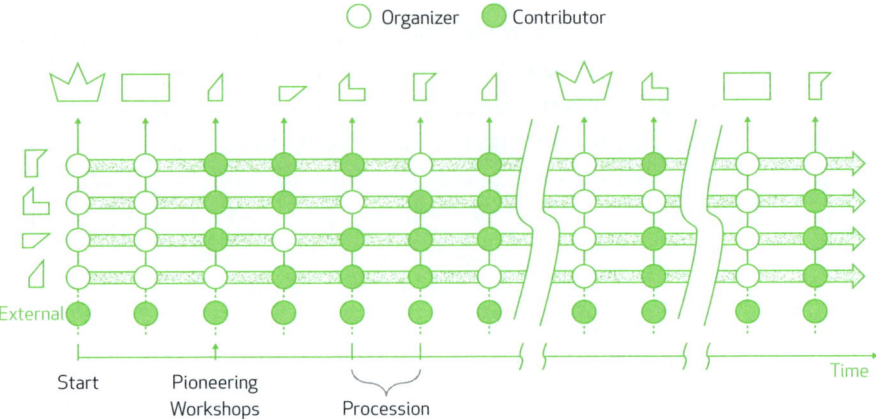

Figure 29 Example of a workshop series of the project in Figure 28, where the shapes in this figure correspond to the shapes in Figure 28. On the left are the workshop participants (the different sub-projects and possible project externals). Every column is "pioneering" workshops with the subject illustrated on the top of the column. The organizer of each workshop is illustrated with a white dot and participants with green dots. Between every workshop every sub-project works to meet the plans (the "procession").

These types of workshops are organized regularly and as needed. The objective is to loop to improve as you go, similar to LEAN's *plan*, *do*, *check* and *act* or Eric Ries' Lean Startup theory[2] with loops of *build*, *measure* and *learn*. You *build* and *re-build* the plan during the workshops. Then you *measure* the plan by working to meet innovative objectives in the plan between the meetings, and as such test the plans feasibility (see "Procession" to effectuate the plans just below). You then complete the loop as you *learn* from the testing and bring the knowledge into the act of updating the plans in a later workshop.

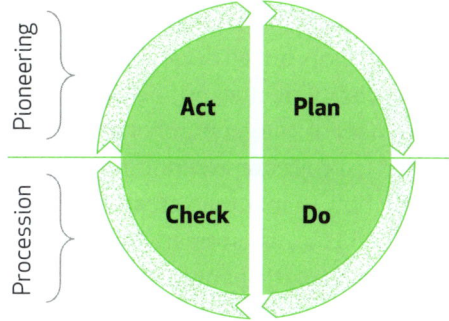

Figure 30   Plan Do Check Act loop with respectively Pioneering and Procession work tasks indicated.

Occasionally in this series of workshops, both the real solution to be delivered and the far future solution are revised and updated based on new knowledge and experience gained as the project matures. This allows the project to keep the long-term focus while maintaining focus on the ongoing activities. In addition to alignment, this also promotes cross functional communication, awareness and cooperation, which again has a positive effect on the ability to change direction, or in other words, project agility. Agility and the extent of the skillset amongst the participants during the workshops makes planning short and effective.

These pioneering workshops are characterized by (see elaboration in *Shepherd leadership and framing the search* on page 85):

- creativity and curiosity
- high acceptance of failure
- low risk focus (in the planning – not to be confused with risk in execution and solution)
- less strong cost focus (of the planning – not the delivered result).

It might be useful to say a few words about how to organize a workshop in order to get the most out of it. A large project may well engage many people, far more than around the five to six people recommended for innovative work (see *Core group members* on page 46). Now, it may not be necessary to involve everyone in the project in every workshop, but all disciplines should be represented. The representative from one discipline may not be the same for every workshop, which allows the involvement of a larger number of people then places available per workshop. In addition to project representatives, other relevant participants should also be invited. So how to maintain creativity in a workshop with 20 to 30 and even up to 40+ participants when creativity is at its best with six people or fewer? The best way is to divide participants in groups of five people and less and make this the main source of creativity (see *Radical innovation as workshops for non-skilled* on page 128). After the creative group work, the workshop gathers in plenum where the result from each group in turn is shared with the rest. In the plenum discussion, the different group proposals are discussed, and particular focus is given to the difference between the suggestions, to make visible the logic behind the different elements and viewpoints. In this way, many good suggestions can make up one or two excellent possibilities.

In very large projects where more than 40 people need to be involved in the planning, there could be several layers of plenum discussions. So, let's say that 160 people are part of the planning, then there can be four parallel sessions with 40 participants in each organized like described above. Then the result from these four parallel sessions can be included in a common session where one result can be extracted in plenum from the four, and as such contain contributions and insight from every participant.

Just like the radical innovation groups (see *Core group members* on page 46), mixing the competence in the group as much as possible and creating multiskilled muscles are important. It may also be an advantage to spend some minutes before group work for everybody to write down all their innovative thoughts and suggestions on paper. If the first part of the group work is to go through every group member's written suggestions, this assures that everyone gets to contribute (and not only the most extroverted person), and it is also an initial boost of creativity hearing all those ideas. This procedure can be used for all parts of the workshop – determining the need, the far future solution, as well as development of the real solution.

"Procession" to effectuate the plans

The Procession follows Pioneering. The systematic innovation work performed during the pioneering workshops needs to be executed. This happens in-between the workshops, and may well be organized in a classic structure, discipline-by-discipline, in a silo style way. The key is that the silo work takes guidance from the pioneering work, which is above and beyond both the silos and the short-term perspective. The tasks coming from the pioneering sessions have anchoring all the way from the ultimate far future solution (guiding direction) via the overall proposed solution (providing a totality perspective) until the different adjacent disciplines (assuring integration). The silo work will therefore not only be *efficient* in the sense that much work can be done in a short time – efficiency is the tendency when you work with fellow colleagues with whom you work daily on similar tasks and often share the same mind-set and habits. The silo work will also be *effective* in the sense that *the right* efforts are made efficiently, since the work is guided by large parts of the involved parties and interest groups considered over a time perspective from present to the far future.

On the contrary to pioneering work, procession work is characterized by:

- Work procedures and obedience
- Strong risk focus
- Strong cost focus
- Low acceptance for failure.

An obvious question at this point is when to do Pioneering and when to move in Procession. Pioneering is needed when the area you enter is not familiar and innovative work is necessary. In the beginning of the project there will necessarily be more innovative work than later on, simply since we learn and make decisions as we go. It also happens to be cheaper when project plan adjustments come earlier so that the impact of the change is smaller. Physical elements are, as an example, way more expensive to change late in a project than the same change on the drawings at the start. It is also likely that the beginning offers innovation work on the overall concept and the main lines along which the project will progress. In order to progress lower level uncertainties, the concept and main lines need to be decided sooner rather than later, and as such uncertainty is replaced by concrete plans. All this will also influence the frequency of the pioneering work and that the time between pioneering workshops will increase to the advantage of procession work. At the same time, the level at which innovation is needed moves from overall concept towards the details. Although more and more of the work becomes procession type work as the level of details in the plans increases, innovation may still be required all the way to the end of the project. As an example, this could be the case if a central module is seriously damaged during transportation just before hand over. This requires pioneering work and may involve many project disciplines and beyond.

More about...

...why middle management has a tendency to become filters stopping radical suggestions to arise in the organization, and why an ambidextrous approach to innovation is needed.

To consider the differences between leadership and management when it comes to innovation, it is essential to understand the different nature of the two quite different tasks associated to each of the positions. As is clear from the title, a company's leadership is meant to lead the way. In competitive environments, there is a constant fight for customers and every player tries to stand out from the crowd in such a way that the customer chooses their product. To find the right strategy under such conditions when leading the way takes creativity and innovative capabilities. They have often an open mind, the ability to keep many options open, are quick to act and ready to adjust or even change direction on short notice if they see a need or an opportunity. Personal skills supporting this character would be elements of creativity, agility, knowledgeability, decisiveness and self-confidence. A good leader would welcome proposals from his or her organization as candidates for the strategic direction, considering these as helpful options for important strategic choices in the future.

Management on the other hand, is not meant to lead the way on a high level. Management's role is to effectuate the strategic decisions made by the leadership and translate them into manageable tasks for the individuals under his or her command, while making sure they have everything they need to accomplish the tasks at hand. Good management can translate orders from above without questioning the content and make these their own and their team's goals. Personal characteristics for management are therefore more in the range of structure, systematic, persistence, knowledge of rules, loyalty and good inter-human skills. In other words, management thinks more in a sequential, linear or waterfall way, contrary to good leadership that thinks laterally.

Now imagine that we have an innovative idea we would like support to pursue. If the idea is of incremental nature, it could be wise to talk to the one in management with the responsibility to deliver on the current field. The likelihood is that this will help him/her achieve his/her goals, which obviously is positive for this person and the managerial tasks. He/she will also have knowledge about the process and might well be able to give the idea high quality assessment, feedback and advice for further work. There may even be funding set aside for an activity offering a similar effect. The leadership would probably not be interested, since this is not his/her responsibility, the task has already been delegated and their ability to give high quality feedback would not be too likely.

Now let us assume that the idea we have is of radical nature. Would it be wise to find the one in management with the responsibility to improve today's solution? Probably not. He/she would have clear objectives to improve the solution at hand, and has no mandate to make the decision to change direction completely. Very often the type of curiosity needed to trigger the interest of a person is not too common within management, because the skills for which they are picked for the position are diagonally different. Furthermore, their expertise and experience may be threatened by the success of the new idea if it is really radical since it will replace the current solution.

The radical idea would probably be better off presented to the leadership. Their mandate is to lead. Good leadership would constantly seek optionality, and radical ideas offer exactly optionality. A leader would be able to put the idea into a strategic connection and see how it relates to other elements in the strategy, which could multiply the value of the idea (or make it irrelevant). Leadership would probably also focus on the core of the radical concept, and leave the details to engineering and further development, since strategy work is more about the main lines.

Metaphorically one can say that management is responsible for delivering a piece of the puzzle, while leadership is searching for better puzzles to play. The variety from which these two can choose is quite different. Management needs the piece that fits the rest. Leadership would consider anything better than what he/she has available at all times.

The mandate of the receiving part of an idea proposal is one of the main reasons why an ambidextrous innovation approach is necessary [5-9]. Incremental ideas are best off following the line up in the organization until it hits someone with the mandate to push the play button. Radical ideas need a totally different route. This route needs to start at a leadership level and needs to end up at the top, where the mandate for changing direction can be found. If such a route is not in place and the radical idea has to go through the middle management layers, it is likely to fail and be stopped. In the unlikely event of a pass, the likelihood is that these middle management levels will twist and tweak the concept, shaping it more into an incremental idea useful for that particular level, and the idea will stop prematurely in the organization (since the one at a leadership level is not too interested in smaller more incremental proposals, which is the reason for delegating that responsibility in the first place), and therefore the radical idea will not meet its full potential.

148 Implement – take out the full value potential

Chapter summary

This chapter is about how to take value out of the flow of radical ideas obviously in a long-term perspective, but also, perhaps less obvious, in the short-term. The main purpose in any time perspective, short or long, is to implement solutions that will allow the company to stay competitive. The very key in this chapter is how radical innovation can create value long before the radical concept will be implemented, if implemented at all. By feeding visions about a possible future to the ongoing incremental projects, and as such move their mental vision or anchor from the previous solution over to an imaginary futuristic situation, the ongoing projects will develop with larger steps, accelerating the innovation pace.

In Lean Startup spirit, longer incremental steps in the direction of the radical concept are excellent "Minimum Viable Product" tests of the radical concept, and as such, the incremental effort reciprocally supports the radical development. It is therefore fair to say that a synergy is achieved between radical and incremental innovation. Dual interdependent innovation is then a reality.

You will hear more about:

- Creating complete future scenarios by prototyping different radical solutions into a totality.
- Selecting the most promising future scenario and communicating it as visions for ongoing incremental projects to generate more stretch in the development, and how this has a LEAN type of effect on development.
- Evaluating the development towards the future scenario and adjusting direction if needed.
- How dual interdependent innovation takes the best of two worlds by developing and implementing radical innovation stepwise with customer feedback throughout the development period.

The aviation industry example

But before we go any further, we should go back to the aviation innovation challenge you were given earlier in the book (see *Build a group and a meeting structure* on page 36). I will now try to explain how I see an optimized aviation industry in the far future. There are many possible directions – here is one:

Basic optimization principles are:

- Safety and reliability
- Low or no manual work
- Energy efficiency
- Time efficiency and machine utilization time (particularly the expensive plane parts)
- On-time delivery.

I can see the following changes based on these optimization principles
Minimum re-load time

1. The plane will be self-flying, which in theory is possible already today. In case any intervention is needed by professionals, this will be remotely controlled by a person or a machine in a hub on the ground.
2. The plane will no longer drive up to a wall and connect to a tunnel, for then to be pushed back out by a second vehicle. Like a bus today the plane will come into a stop and continue in the same direction without external help (see Figure 31).
3. Everything the plane needs to continue to next destination will be ready for a quick exchange with the elements the plane delivers at the current destination, which includes passengers, cargo, energy and possible modularized spare parts (see Figure 32).

   a. The planes payload and consumables body will be detachable from the engine, wing and controls section, similar to how cargo containers can be loaded onto a truck or a train today in a matter of seconds. This will allow many things, one of which is preloading and post off-loading of cargo and passengers without delaying

the flight schedule. The preloaded energy unit could be a separate unit, making up the totality with the loaded "cartridge" ready to take off in a very short time.
- b Before the motorized part of the plane arrives passengers will carry their own luggage into their reserved section of the planes payload body (cartridge) located possibly below ground at this point. In a similar way cargo and energy will be loaded.

4 When the plane arrives all arriving payload will be exchanged with all departing elements in a matter of seconds.

- a Incoming body will be exchanged with the departing body.
- b Energy (battery or hydrogen-based fuel) can be loaded in the same way, because the docking station type refilling simply takes too much time.
- c If any piece of the motorized part or any other part of the plane have given notice by remote communication during the trip that it needs control or replacement, the entire module, in a newly restored mode, will be waiting and exchanged with the one containing the "complaining" piece.
- d The short stop will allow the motors to stay hot throughout the ground stop and the internal temperature variations will reduce, allowing tighter tolerances and as a result higher efficiency.

5 In case of motor breakdown in the air, the plane body will detach from the motor and energy part. This will be deaccelerated using for example a parachute-type solution which will bring it gently back to ground, while it sends out signals for help and communicates its location. The body is floating in case the plane is over the sea. The motor part of the plane will make use of whatever function remains to maneuver its way to a non-populated or at least minimum damage crash site.

6 Passengers will not separate from their luggage but carry it themselves both into their reserved section of the plane and off again. There will

no longer be a need to hand it in just to wait to pick it back up again afterwards. They can also find their seats at their own convenience.
7   No de-icing necessary any longer due to the very short time on the ground.

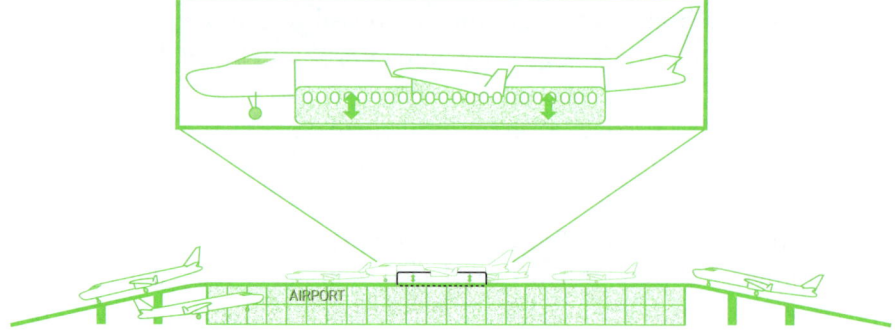

Figure 31   Sketch of a possible future airport according to the proposal in this example. The planes come in from the right, pass over the terminal, offload all disembarking elements in one cartridge and immediately reload the embarking elements for a minimum stop duration, before it continues to the left for departure. In the illustration, the runway is parallel to the service lane with the terminal, but landing, service and departure could also be on a line for one continuous flow.

There are probably many other possible future aviation scenarios. But let us for a moment say that this is the one we believe in. If you were in charge of a new airport to be built, which improvements would you have proposed to make sure your airport would be prepared for the future?

Now, look up the answers you had in Chapter 2 on the next big thing in the aviation industry. This was your answer before you had a peek into a possible future scenario within aviation. Which of the two proposals steps are furthest into the future? Did you feel that insight into a possible far future scenario made you stretch further and propose a longer first step?

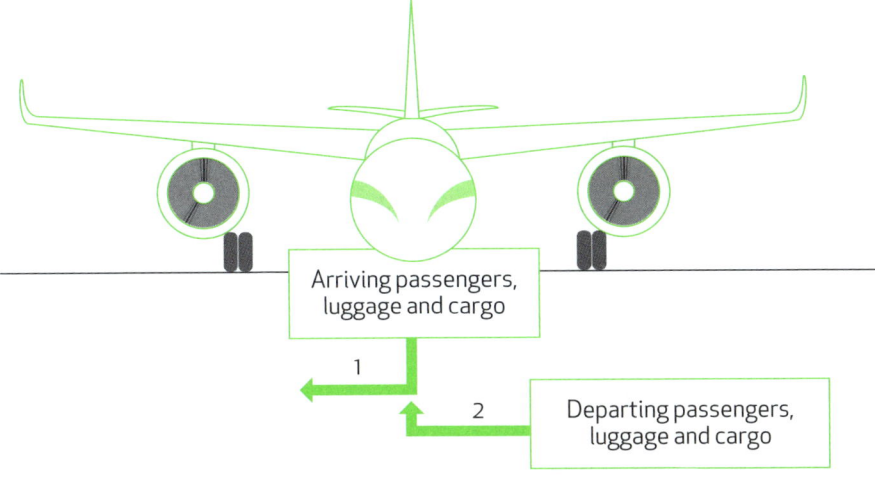

Figure 32 The principle of disembarking and embarking a plane fast by replacing the passenger section with luggage, cargo and supply in a cartridge type of replacement system.

Radical innovation not only for tomorrow but also today

Surviving is a struggle for many companies. Development pace is so high that all the spare capacity, the capacity not busy with daily production, is totally occupied with the next move. Often there is no time to look further into the horizon. It is not that looking takes so much time, but the risk of being wrong is high and the payback-time is so far out. And even if your future perspective would not be wrong, most companies find it tremendously challenging to implement new thinking into a traditional structure. There is a natural resistance to making significant changes, which inherently will influence a large number of people. So many companies struggle to implement their radical ideas and therefore don't bother making future outlooks either. This chapter will argue that both risk and payback-time can be significantly reduced while the general acceptance to change reaches a new higher level, if the cards are played right at this point.

We have seen how radical ideation can be produced and reproduced systematically in a cheap and effective way giving real results. We have also seen that a broad effort will create a flow of future options, a flow, which can be gathered on a leadership level without being de-risked and stripped for those essential fundamental change propositions on the way if some simple measures are taken on the route to the top. And at the top we have spoken about how visual models of complete future scenarios can be built composing lots of single concept proposals (innovative bricks) of different impact classes. But then what? Let's say that one future scenario stands out as more realistic and attractive than the others. It fits with the company profile and the competence needed is within reach. How to advance from here? How to build enthusiasm and how to create a general acceptance?

The obvious possibility is to start preparing for going in this direction recruiting from those already interested in this way of thinking. Start with the low hanging fruit and develop, take the time it takes and dive into this endless market – engage the change agents[18]. Create products, processes, procedures and services to educate the customer, and expand bit by bit, slowly "cannibalizing" the present solutions as they become outcompeted. Indeed this is a way to go, but it takes time, it costs money, the risk is high and return on investment will materialize many years later, at least not before the performance dip in the "S"-curve has been recovered (see Figure 5), if at all.

Let's look at an example to illustrate this position: Let's say that we make cars, standard diesel and petrol cars. We even have an electrical alibi to ramp up our green profile and be prepared if this market takes off. Our best radical scenario, however, tells us that in the future the cars will drive themselves (which has probably been the case for many car companies around the world for quite some years now). How to deal with that? See also illustrations in Figure 33, where a box is believed to be the result of long-term incremental development seen in Figure 33 A, and a vision of this start to be clear already now after systematic radical innovation shown as a flashlight in Figure 33 B.

One obvious possibility in the case with the self-driving car vision case is to realize a prototype of the radical suggestion, develop a self-driving car, and try the concept out on the market. This will reveal how the customer would receive it. On the other hand, this would also be the risky, long and expensive development route, even for the simplest and smallest version of the self-driving car. Just imagine how many non-proven components, systems and processes need to be added to the car for it to drive safely and reliably. In addition, when this project is finished, even if you are first out – or rather *particularly* if you are first out – many things may have happened between your decision and the release. And even if nothing did, perhaps this would be a too large step for the customer and they might need some "education" or at least time to embrace the new solution, something you may not have predicted and therefore pose an additional cost/delay. Anyway, self-driving cars will come, so with persistence, this might well have paid off eventually.

There is a parallel road that can give benefit much faster. If you took your self-driving car concept down to the team that develops the next model car, a model in your range, choosing a suitable model for a customer who would be interested in self-driving cars sometime in the future. You show them your wild ideas, put it in context and explain why you believe this could be the future of cars many years from now. Maybe they even have opinions here. Then you ask them how *they think* the next model will look if it took the first step in the direction of the future concept. Perhaps ask them which elements they think would be feasible in a short time perspective. In fact, you ask them for advice, because one thing is to predict the large development lines, a totally different thing is to materialize elements of this development as real components and services in real cars in a short time perspective *and* make it beneficial at the same time.

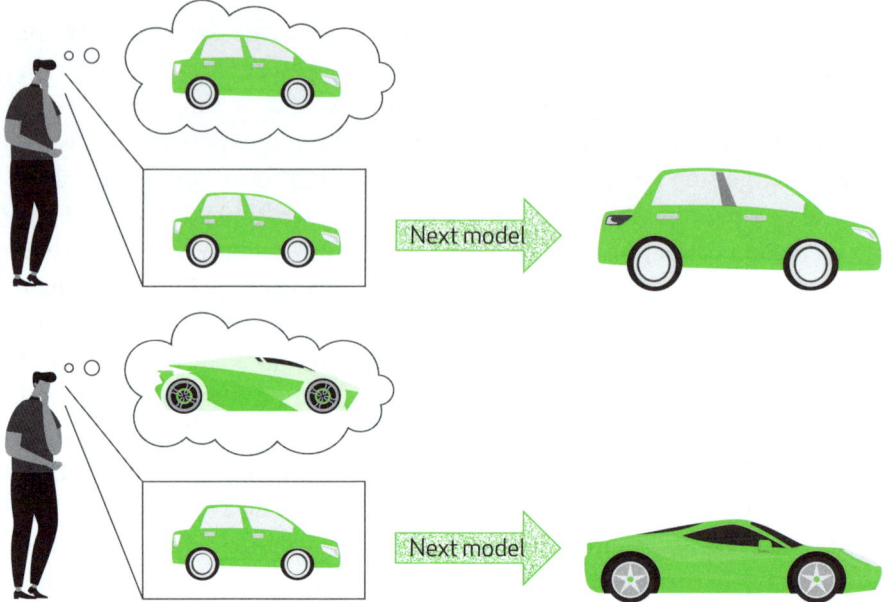

By approaching the developers in this way, you would move their mental anchor from the last existing version of the model they worked with onto the future concept. A mental anchor in this case is a term introduced by psychologist and Nobel Prize winner Daniel Kahneman[1], an example of which can be illustrated in the sales process of a used motorbike. When the seller says how much he wants for the motorbike (for example the amount he writes in the advertisement), this amount will become a mental anchor throughout the sales process, and all adjustments thereafter will be related to this first mental anchor. Now back to the self-driving car example. When the previous car model is the mental anchor, we see what we have seen just too many times that only a few subtle design changes are made, perhaps a couple of nuances in a few colors of the color scheme, some rounded corners in the design and a slightly stronger engine version with a fraction lower consumption which will be totally blown out of proportions in the ads. This is a bit like walking forward in unfamiliar territory with your eyes and your front-side facing backwards (towards the previous model) – you only see the path you have passed. However, when the mental anchor is a solution from the future, it is not easy to say what the changes will be, but they will most likely end up being significant (far from marginal). It is simply human nature to stretch further when the goal is clear, visible and challenging, and if in addition it is realistic and logical, but unreachable in the short perspective, the development pace will increase from day one (see this illustrated in Figure 33 C). In a "Need-based innovation" perspective (see More about on page 56), we can say that the development team replaces their contemporary need with a futuristic one. From the iceberg theory we can see the power of changes aligned with our basic beliefs and convictions (see Figure 40). Meeting these basics values in people can literally move mountains, particularly within innovation. Seen in this light, driverless cars may not mobilize full development motivation in everyone. Although driverless cars may make taxi rides cheaper, more available, safer and improve efficiency by counteracting queuing, this will probably raise fundamental questions like employment and fear of losing control of the car. Nevertheless, even without 100% contribution from the soft values in the body of the iceberg, the car development team would certainly have increased the development pace significantly compared to a situation without a clear view of the future scenario. This example is meant to illustrate that a clearly communicated realistic radical concept can make the ongoing incremental concepts *increase the advancement pace*, just like you hopefully felt with the next development step within the aviation industry without and then with this future concept available.

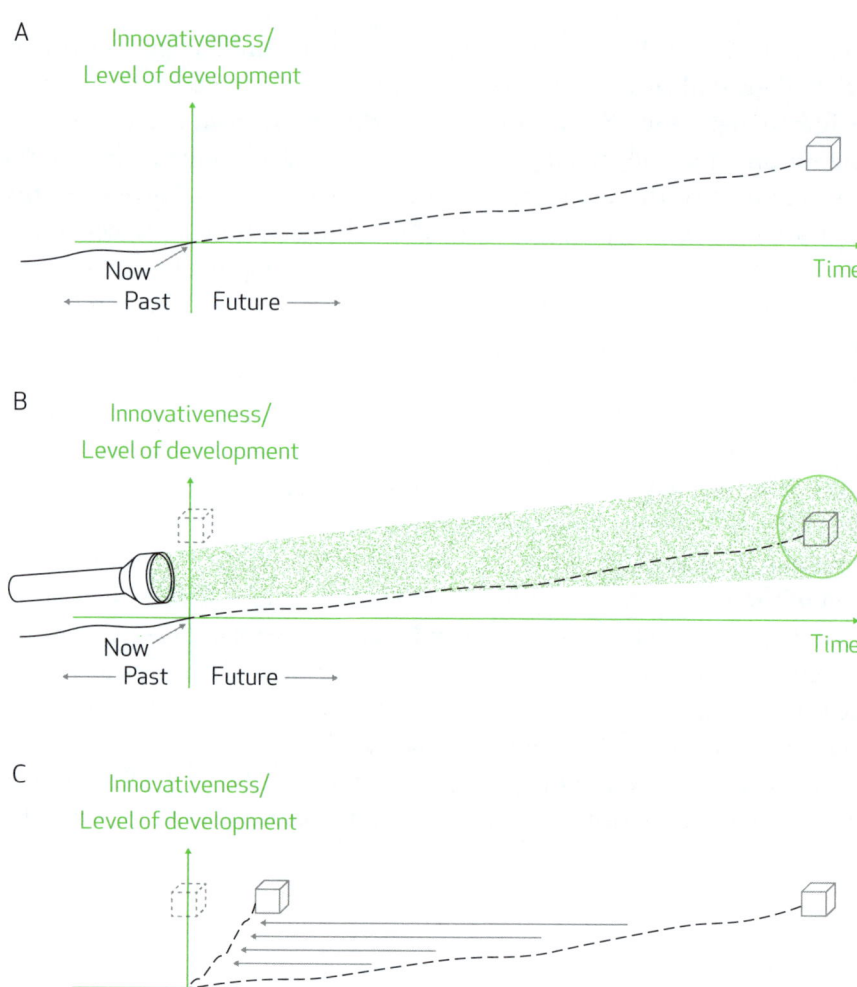

Figure 33 A) illustrates a development stage in the future represented by a dice-shaped block that would come about a particular time in the future by following natural incremental development represented by the dashed line. In figure B) we look successfully into the future, for example with a radical innovation effort, and get a vision about the future now (the dashed block). This allows us to increase the pace, jump many intermediate increments, and bring forward the future at an earlier stage, shown in C).

Another great effect of this method is how it also addresses an effect that should not be underestimated; the "Not Invented Here" effect[3]. Not-Invented-Here effect refers to the room between the motivation an individual or a team feels for lifting an idea or solution up when they have been a part of developing the idea/solution and when they have not. Not-invented-here greatly influences motivation. In a case where the development team would be handed a solution to implement, the tendency is that they would have taken a critical position. In the case where they are asked for advice, asked to propose how to approach a possible trend and they actually come up with a proposal, they would mobilize all possible energy to make their own proposal work. This also allows stakeholders around them to take on a critical role and let the team defend their proposals, with the potential to lift the product even further. The Not-Invented-Here syndrome should not be underestimated.

Real value is generated when radical innovation meets incremental.

The extent to which the car industry actually has taken this approach or not is unknown to the author. However, the development has taken a direction as if this method would have been used. Cars have constantly been updated with equipment which appears to be building blocks for safe driverless driving, each offering individually a small additional benefit to the customer, at the same time as they eventually will make up an indispensable part of the radical ultimate goal: driverless cars, which totally change the way to get from A to B. These technologies are things like parking sensors, self-parking systems, dead zone sensors, road marking detectors, distance measurements between cars, GPS orientation capabilities, active brake assistance and much more. All these things have added a small advantage to the customer when it has been offered as a new feature in a car, but they all play a role in preparing cars to drive fully by themselves. This is radically changing the car industry in small incremental steps.

It is indeed interesting to see this in light of Eric Ries' Lean Startup theory[2]. His advice would surely be not to make the perfect solution before you enter the market, which in this case refers to not kicking off the prototype of the fully functional self-driving car from day one. He would certainly advise to make a Minimum Viable Product (MVP), which could be similar to the way the car industry is approaching this issue; adding features that would bring you in the preferred direction slowly and steadily, allowing you to learn on the way and make those important adjustments (pivots) as the need for them surfaces, which means building confidence through technology iteration. The proposal in this book, though, is about how to generate and apply a vision about the future, or let's say the endpoint, as a guiding star for change by practically motivating larger steps in the right direction. In the same way as the MVP exposed to real customers guides further product development, and just as a company strategy occasionally is reviewed and adjusted, the vision can be adjusted as you go, too, to account for more experience and learning on the way (see Figure 35).

The effect we are discussing here is about making some predictions about the future. When communicating these predictions in the right way to those involved with development and production of the present solution, this will positively affect the development of the present solutions. It will increase the development pace. You may say that our future outlook will *come back* to the present and positively affect our current efforts, somewhat like a boomerang turns and physically comes back. That is why I refer to this pace increase as the *Boomerang effect of radical innovation*. You could argue that we actually replace the current perceived needs (see More about page 56) with a prospective future need in the form of a viable future scenario.

The Boomerang effect makes the future come sooner.

At this point it is worth reflecting on how the boomerang effect uses *justify in* and *justify out* (see Work method for radical innovation on page 66) strategically to increase the innovation pace. In standard incremental innovation where the mental anchor is the present solution, justify out is applied, which limits the step out length by demanding argumentation to change something. We also spoke about the importance of applying justify in when making the ultimate future concept, which motivates a large step out length by building a new concept from scratch. However, when feeding the future concept back to the doer team and motivating them to materialize the concept in a shorter time perspective, you go back to apply justify out. In this way you motivate as little step out as possible from the future concept. Or perhaps it is more explanatory to replace "step out" with "step back" in this case. By applying justify out from the ultimate concept, the development team needs to argue why they moderate elements of the futuristic concept, which effectively reduce the step back and assures stretch compared to the present solution. This is key to achieve the desired stretch effect.

I am often asked if clear visions about the future can be dangerous because as they guide everyone towards a target, they also take the focus away from the alternatives. My experience is almost diametrically different. When you try to prepare the ground for a group of innovative people by saying that there are two principally different solution spaces for a certain challenge, they would immediately critically challenge this statement by looking for other often more exotic possible solution spaces that can be added to the two stated. My experience is that an attempt to start the innovative process by analyzing the solution space or even suggesting solutions increases creativity rather than limiting it (see *Facilitator tasks before the meeting* starting on page 38). The same principle applies for a future mental anchor. This will guide people in a direction and get them up to speed fast, at the same time as they will challenge the statement and look around the mental anchor to see if the optimum can be found elsewhere. See this illustrated in Figure 34 A, where the targeted radical innovation shown as a flashlight reveals that the future solution might not be the box we started to develop, but rather a pyramid in a slightly different direction. Searching and testing will give new insight, so the mental anchors and the future scenario need revision from time-to-time. In this way the visual objective will be no more than semi-static. It will iterate into something better as insight evolves and grows (see Figure 34 B where the development has been adjusted and a pyramid is in place long before the incremental path would get there).

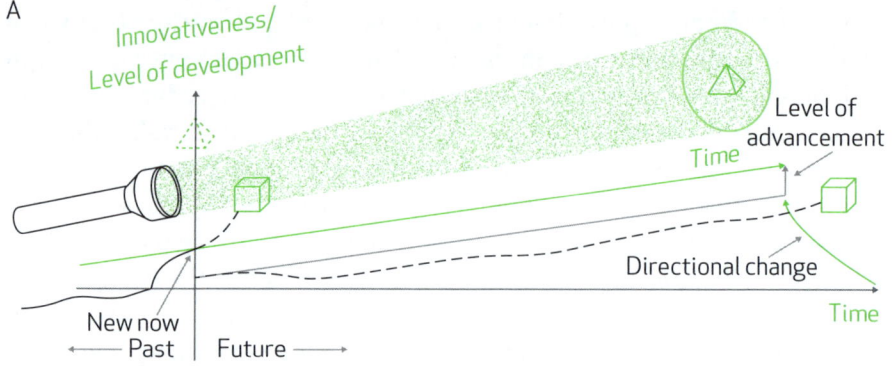

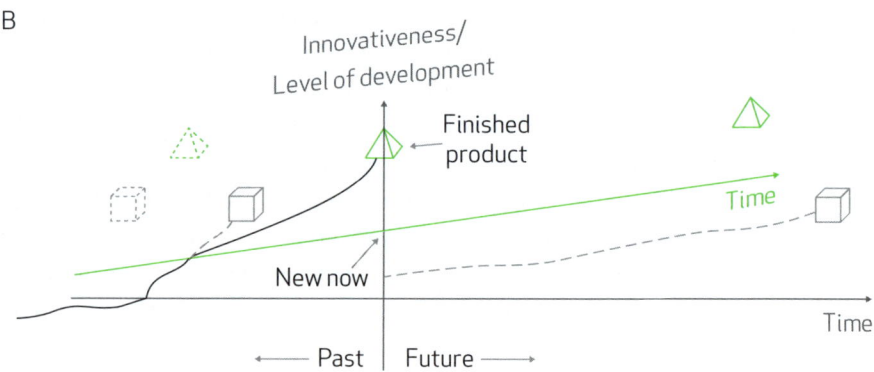

Figure 34 Iterative process applied on the case in Figure 33: After having worked to develop the dice-shaped block, a new future outlook is performed in A) revealing a change in direction (the green axis) where the solution now is adjusted to a pyramid. The development shift from grey to green line to meet the new target in B) and the pyramid is developed, well adapted to the latest outlook.

Iterating the future mental anchor (the radical concept) to something more optimal with growing insight from the experience with stretch in the incremental projects, means that there is a mutual benefit between incremental and radical innovation following this method. Not only can the radical concepts help the pace in the incremental work, but the stepped-up incremental work can also guide the radical concept. The incremental and the radical innovation can mutually benefit each other. Therefore, reaching this point, the company can say they have achieved synergy between incremental and radical innovation.

 If you can't get innovation right, go left.

However, to unleash this potential in the organization, the involved leadership, management and other stakeholders need to appreciate the ultimate solutions far into the future. From the last paragraph of *Philosophy for creating radical ideas* starting on page 62 we saw that risky and uncertain visions like this can be quite difficult for management to support. Risky projects that might never be realized are quite opposite to what they are appreciated to deliver regularly. However, at this point in the process it is important for those who feel discomfort to get intermediately out of their comfort zone and explore beyond. The good news is that in the next phase, after the ultimate concept is fed back to the doers, then leadership, management and other stakeholders can go back into their comfort zone, with focus on practical near-term feasibility and risk management as the doers now try to sell them their implementable solution. Then the process is back to standard incremental practice, although with larger development steps.

Portfolio example

Supporting organizational change process
Some years ago, around 2014, the oil prices saw a historically dramatic drop from well over 100 US dollars per barrel to as low as into the twenties. Long before this drop, Equinor's CEO and his team started an

efficiency project to better adapt the company to the volatile oil price regime experienced and the dwindling margins even in periods with high prices. This project had the mandate to change quite large parts of how the company ran the business, including a major reorganization. Particularly the cost side of the revenue was under their attention.

My little radical innovation group decided to help out without any invitation to do so. We skipped all the analysis of the current situation, and saved lots of time with this move, compared to the formal change project which was named Statoil Technical Efficiency Project (STEP) – Equinor was named Statoil at the time. Instead of analyzing the current situation, we looked way into the future and discussed how an energy company with roots in the oil and gas sector would look in a future where profits might be marginal. Before jumping to solutions, we decided to take inspiration from an industry that has been marginal for a long time; the airline industry. Like ours, this industry also has a strong safety culture since an accident would be catastrophic for those involved as well as the whole company. The core of safety culture in both these industries is flawless handwork from both operational and maintenance crews, and seamless communication between the two. So after having spent some time with core people from the STEP project to better understand the challenge at hand, we brought in the leader of the pilot union from the airline company with the highest on-time delivery at the time (fewest delays compared to predicted schedule) – they had made tremendous progress on this important performance indicator. We hoped for an informal chat and got a real eye opener. We were given a good overview of the important processes they had gone through to get to these excellent numbers, how safety and effectivity had to go hand-in-hand, what went well and what was more challenging through this journey. Funnily enough, both parties were surprised after the meeting how much two companies in two very different industrial segments had so many things in common with respect to challenges associated with the strive for progress.

After this successful meeting we started to work with how we would propose our company should be organized in the future. Also experience from other marginal businesses, aluminum extrusion and shipping, from which our own members had first-hand knowledge, were woven into our solutions. There were organizational suggestions, particularly on how to distribute power and responsibility, expert and knowledge distribution/support, the power balance between production (operations) and the ability to produce (maintenance), but also other aspects for organization of responsibility. There were also suggestions about cultural and mentality issues like failure support vs. condition monitoring and best practice vs. continuous improvement, as well as safety reporting and follow up. We "wrapped it up" and sent it!

At first our report surprised the receiving part of the STEP project. Since we were uninvited to the table, they didn't expect any report like this from anyone, and particularly not one touching many of the central discussion areas they had going at the time (which was to an extent coincidental). After the initial surprise, any concern for parallel and competing efforts within the same company was replaced by positive curiosity, and we simply turned to our next challenge and the STEP project could choose whether to take our input into account or brutally ditch it at their own convenience. Years later I was, however, told that our work had played a role and gave birth to some inspiration. On what and how much, I don't know and honestly don't need to know either. We wanted to practice *the boomerang effect of radical innovation* and simply help in a challenging situation.

Another more technical example of the boomerang effect came about in the example shared in the end of *Timing* on page 100. About two years after the subsea solution was spread around amongst our in-house experts within this technology area and parked in the archive, a new version of the same principle was suggested, developed and installed multiple times. The solution *we* had proposed had to be implemented on new subsea systems. The new version that came up within the subsea team, was a practical and really elegantly simple solution that could be retrofitted to subsea systems already in place. A truly creative and excellent solution far from our subsea solution, but based on the same principles. I guess both solutions, in particular the latter

> one implemented numerous times, helped put focus on this solution space guiding further development that way. From a radical innovation point of view, to me this was an example of *the boomerang effect* when the radical solution itself was a bit too much for one step.

Dual interdependency – the best of both worlds

When radical innovation is used to guide and stretch the largest innovation muscle in the company, the incremental innovation muscle, and the resulting increased pace in incremental innovation in return can guide radical innovation, the new combined effect gets the best of both worlds (see Figure 35). I refer to this as dual interdependency, which is an advanced form of ambidextrous innovation (interdependent ambidexterity to be more precise, but that is both complicated to pronounce and sounds strange). This dual interdependent innovation offers safe steps based on knowledge and data, improvement in every step de-risked by customer feed-back, and it meets *invented here*[3] in all parts of the company, just like incremental innovation efforts do. It offers return on investment in a relatively short time frame, also like incremental innovation. At the same time dual interdependent innovation offers increased development speed in a targeted direction based on sound judgements about the future, just like radical innovation. It offers higher rewards as the solutions improve faster, accompanied with a more competitive company profile, also just like radical innovation.

Dual interdependent innovation is the best of both worlds.

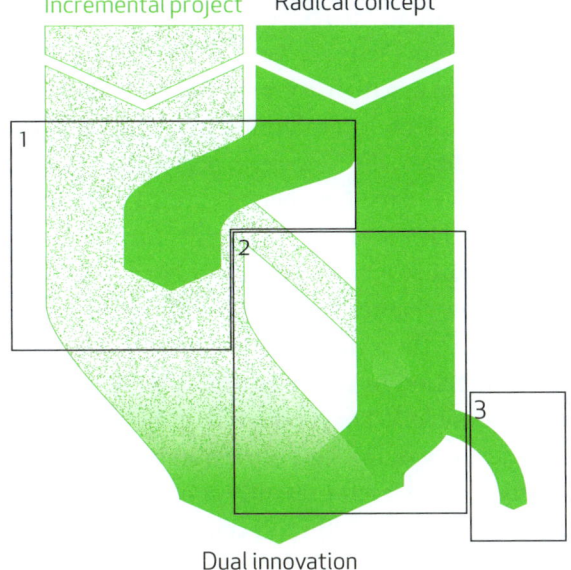

Figure 35 This illustration is a continuation of the ambidexterity seen in Figure 27 on page 128, and shows how radical concepts and incremental projects can interact and make each other better (Dual interdependent Innovation). Box 1: Illustrates the Boomerang Effect which causes the incremental concept to stretch when guided by a relevant radical concept. Box 2: Shows how the experience with the stretching incremental project can give valuable feedback which adjusts the radical concept. Box 3: Indicates that the new insight can create yet another radical concept, which potentially can start the loop again by yet another Boomerang Effect.

This healthy playfulness where radical and incremental innovation can play better with each other stands out as very different to what I too often see when future plans are being made. Roadmaps divided into short, medium and long-term plans often seem to start at the wrong end. The short-term perspective is perceived as the easiest, which is a continuation of the ongoing activities, and therefore the first one to enter the future plans. Second are the medium-term perspectives since these are what naturally follows the ongoing activities. This takes some more effort, but not too much since it is generally about concretizing existing ideas and thoughts about the next step that have emerged during the ongoing activities. Last out and perceived as being most complicated are the long-term plans. Long-term plans are associated with superficial concepts in a vague context which means a high degree of risk and uncertainty, all of which quite often make management uncomfortable (see *Philosophy for creating radical ideas* on page 62). In addition, the long-term perspective needs to be a natural continuation of the short and medium perspective, to make the whole roadmap realistic (which in itself takes away any possibility for a new direction). This is arguably adapting the future to your plans, rather than adapting the plans to the expected future. This chapter, in fact the entire book, proposes the latter; to start the road map with the long-term plans. The obvious reason is that any expected change of direction in the far future needs to be incorporated into the plans as soon as possible. What good is it that the short and medium-term plans take you comfortably in the "left" direction if the future turns out to be in the "right" direction, even if left presently appears fairly logical?

In this context it could be useful to elaborate on a company's ability to innovate and split performance into three different levels. The first and simplest level is when future plans and progress start in the present solutions and stretch forward from there. This normally leads to incremental innovation and the essential continuous improvement of the existing income base, but it doesn't offer the ability to challenge the prevailing direction and offer new products and services. The second level is when the company handles ambidexterity in the sense that there are two different routes for incremental and radical innovation, which allow radical ideas to survive and ultimately challenge the present products, services and direction. The third and most advanced level is when the company manages dual interdependency where the incremental and the radical efforts, which indeed generally follow different routes in the company, can interact and play each other better; the radical concepts inspire the incremental efforts to stretch, while the increased incremental progress stimulate the radical development and growth. This require a deep and mature innovative culture over large parts of the organization, which leads us straight to the subject of the last chapter starting on the next page.

170 Incentives and culture – make sustainable growth

Chapter summary

This chapter is about how to build an innovative company culture promoting sustainable growth, and how incentives are a key enabler to achieve this. In an innovation perspective, it is useful to consider three groups with somewhat different interests, interfaces and view angles to innovation, for both the incentive and the culture part. These three groups are respectively the Idea Proposer, the Idea Receiver and the Passive Users (see Figure 36). The groups' different approach to innovation call for different incentive systems and even different means to build an innovative culture within each group.

In this chapter you will hear more about:

- How incentive systems need to promote cooperation, and that "the winner takes it all" does not serve that purpose.
- How incentive systems for idea proposers with advantage can be disconnected individual ideas and be more related to innovative activity over time (like other promotions in companies).
- How efficient incentives can vary between countries, and industries all the way down to individuals.
- How innovation activity logged through an ERP system can make the incentive system more transparent and measurable, be an asset to all parties directly involved in innovation and be a valuable tool for statistics.
- How the most important part to promote efficient reception of ideas around the organization is to take away the barriers, barriers such as resources being fully tied up and making it difficult to take up ideas between portfolio reviews.
- How it could be good for idea implementation if innovative suggestions stand out from the pre-planned portfolio with for example their own color in evaluation documents, and that a healthy balance between the two is recognized.
- How incentives for the passive end users of innovation, next to negative incentives such as avoiding losing the job, are about communicating and involving everyone early.
- How culture building is a question of:

    - Treating people's ideas with respect whether these are worth continuing or not
    - Lifting up both successful new ideas and associated inventors in the public domain for inspiration, organizational idea anchoring and increased overall involvement
    - Creating a company structure allowing new promising concepts to be taken up as formal projects on a regular basis
    - Setting targets and promoting development in directions aligned with (or at least not directly opposing) peoples' values, beliefs and world views.

Some basics before approaching incentives and culture building

To consider an incentive system and start effective culture building it is worth considering which groups are involved in the innovation process and their role to make innovation succeed. In this context we can consider three different groups

1. Idea proposer: A person involved in developing new ideas and concepts, and, as such, is a part of the creative team coming up with the idea and proposing it to the rest of the company. The proposer can work as an individual or as a part of a team.
2. Idea receiver: A person involved on the receiver side of the process, who in one way or another formally or informally has some sort of administrative role which includes understanding an idea developed by someone else and giving (or not giving) acceptance through supporting the idea and assisting in further organizational anchoring. This is normally a high number of people all the way from the first touchpoint beyond the proposers, for example the proposer's office companion, and all the way to the one responsible for accepting the product for use for the "n^{th} time".
3. Passive user: All the rest – all those who are neither idea proposers nor receivers, but are still indirectly associated with any and all innovations by sharing the company risk (positive and negative) and having to adjust to any changes the innovation might impose whether it succeeds and gets implemented or fails.

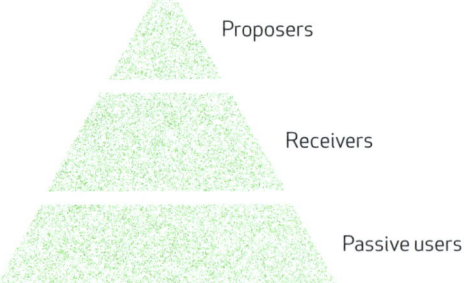

Figure 36   Three principally different groups involved in the innovation process, sharing the positive and negative risk associated to the changes innovation offers and imposes.

These three groups look at innovation from three different angles and the tendency is that the three groups act differently throughout the innovation process. It can therefore be useful to separate these three groups when incentives and culture are to be discussed.

Incentives promoting cooperation

To construct a sustainable innovation culture, a key enabler is a well-functioning incentive system. Incentives in innovation context could be monetary/salary, recognition, freedom to innovate, freedom in general work, time off, budgets to innovate, titles, job security and much more.

The effect of each incentive will vary across different cultures around the world, in different industries/companies, at different levels in the company, including down to individuals. For example, in some countries like the USA, the differences in salary levels are high and individuals who are in a position where they can act successfully in creative teams may already be fairly high on the salary scale in society. On the other hand, result pressure and competition may demand long work hours and stress. In this environment monetary incentives may be less effective, but freedom to explore, recognition or time off may be more motivating. In other parts of the word, like in the Scandinavian countries, the internal barriers between employees on one side and the different managerial and leadership layers on the other are lower. An employee's freedom to influence his/her everyday tasks is high, while the salary system across society is for many surprisingly flat. Under such conditions, there may be more motivation in monetary incentives and less in work freedom. In yet other parts of the world, the social class systems stand strong, like Japan, recognition may be a strong motivator. You have to find which motivator fits your environment and try to "play those strings".

In the following we will look at incentive systems for Idea Proposers, idea Receivers and Passive Users. We will look more at the interesting differences between these groups with respect to innovation culture under the heading *Building a sustainable innovation culture for growth* later in this chapter. At this point it will be enough to say that the different groups mentioned need different incentive systems.

Incentive systems for the Idea Proposers

When it comes to incentive systems, there are indeed differences around the world that needs to be considered. However, some effects are universal. Innovation is always better when individuals share openly and cooperate to achieve even more (searching for synergy). The incentive system should support cooperation, or, as a minimum, not counteract cooperation. An example of a poor incentive system with a negative effect on cooperation is competition like sport events where the best gets the prize. Under these conditions one competitor will seriously hesitate to help a fellow competitor on his/her innovation project simply because this will reduce his/her own chances to win. At a very minimum, such competition should reward all proposals over a certain limit, even if such a limit can be challenging to communicate clearly up front. If more than one can win or even better, everyone above a certain stated limit, one is likely to help another because the other would then be more likely to help in return, and they would both increase their winning chances.

Incentives within innovation are indeed challenging, because cooperation will improve the result at the same time as a healthy competitive spirit can mobilize energy for many participants to make the necessary extra effort. Rewarding everyone over a certain limit can also be challenging. Let's say that a team (e.g. an innovation group) comes up with a promising idea. To come up with the proposed result they have invited some individuals from outside the group to get access to expertise they didn't possess themselves. In addition, members of the group have spoken informally to colleagues on the matter, who have given some contributions, but for the most on peripheral matters. Also, in this imaginary case, one of the core members took the role as a critic, challenging the rest to improve on the weak parts of the concept, without actually having direct inventive contributions in this case, but guiding the team onto an exciting solution. Another member, the one who brought the challenge to the table, came up with much of the specific inventive contributions him/herself. This is not an unrealistic sequence of events. Who to reward in this case? The fixed group only, or perhaps all those formally invited? How about the contributors from the informal discussions? Should the reward be flat? This type of direct reward system is very hard if not impossible to get fair. Also, to get anywhere near a fair direct reward system it takes a high level of administration.

There are indeed many reward systems around, and some may also be good. I will propose a system that I feel meets many of the challenges described above, and can be perceived as a fair system by the users. The administrative loads are not too heavy either.

However, before suggesting an incentive system, it might be worth mentioning that the main purpose of the incentive system is to balance out the parts of the innovation process that generally are perceived as negative so there is an overall drive to get involved in the innovation process and propose ideas. Those things normally perceived as negative could be:

1. Professionality exposure – present an idea you perceive as new to the world (at least to the company) to a team of idea receivers, who often possess an expertise within the subject in question, with the risk that they can pinpoint obvious show stoppers that will kill the idea directly leaving the proposer in a bad light.
2. Uncertainty – arguing for an idea at a very early stage, which is not particularly comprehensively described and without confirmative testing, that you may not be too sure of yourself (the probability to be misunderstood or simply to be proven wrong).
3. Extra work – administrative work related to idea description, registration, information packages and so on.
4. Low probability for success.

The proposed incentive system disconnects rewards from specific ideas and focuses on general innovation activity. This means no direct idea reward system. Similar to a standard general promotion system, innovation can be recognized through promotions in an *innovation promotion system*. The system can have a number of levels (title examples: innovator, senior innovator chief innovator and so on), where promotion from one level to the next releases more rewards, just like other promotional systems. These rewards need to be adapted to what motivates people in this particular company, with reference to the above described differences in motivation according to country, industry and so on. As an example, one could imagine that the different levels formally release time and budget to spend on innovation, which increases with increasing promotion level. In an innovation context, such rewards can be divided into two groups, rewards that enhance further innovation activity and other rewards.

Rewards enhancing innovation activity could be:

1. Budget dedicated for innovation work
2. Time dedicated innovation work
3. Freedom to influence which innovative projects to pursue
4. Association to or membership in special innovation groups
5. Direct access to mentors and key idea receivers
6. Direct access to test facilities.

Other rewards could be:

1. Title
2. Recognition (priority parking, "hall of fame", publicity, office location etc.)
3. Salary increase (permanent or not permanent)
4. Bonus (one off)
5. Time off/extra holiday.

But these lists can obviously be far longer. In addition, comes the overall incentive, which is to be associated with a successful idea that has gone all the way to implementation where it brings about clear improvements.

It is of vital importance for a promotional reward system linked to innovation activity to log innovation activity somehow, to measure progress and to help associate innovation to people. Such a system could be an ERP (Enterprise Resource Planning) system adapted to innovation (see More about below).

More about...

...how an Enterprise Resource Planning (ERP) system could benefit the administration of innovation work.

To enhance the administrative handling of innovation in a company, a possibility would be to introduce an ERP (Enterprise Resource Planning) type of system for innovation activity. ERP systems use database technology to store relevant data and extract necessary information from this data.

This could offer innovators updated status on all their innovation activities at any time, including available budgets, funding spent, historical data, coming decision gates, requirements associated with the next stage gate, deadlines, decision makers and whatever the company finds worth entering into the system and share.

It offers the administrating team an efficient platform to communicate with the inventors and keep an updated overview over the active and historical innovation portfolio a mouse click or two away.

However, this also offers the company a way to extract statistics about innovation progress across the company, and how the organization responds to the efforts being made – what works and what does not. These statistics can be the foundation for promotions and as such increase both the transparency and predictability of the process.

I am often asked how collective innovation progress can be measured. The dilemma is that the results themselves cannot be measured alone, because the time it takes to get from an idea to a finished implemented product takes too long, so improvement iteration loops would take far too long. On the other hand, measuring incoming ideas would only give a measure of a small part of the innovation process, and this number will not be representative for the whole innovation process. A good solution would be to log all the steps from when an idea is formally registered until it either is stopped or is implemented, like an ERP system could offer. This will allow constant monitoring of the entire process and the contribution from all parties involved.

 What you measure, you improve.

> But equally important and valuable: An ERP system could also be used as a tool to mobilize handpicked innovative task force initiatives based on active innovation activity, if circumstances would demand such efforts. This could, for example, be useful in a critical situation and particularly in case the situation is urgent. This can be a great asset for any company.
>
> Far simpler systems than full ERP-systems would also work for the purpose, and a fairly large company could come far with simple excel sheets as well.

A promotion system on innovation activities introduces certain advantages compared to more idea specific recognition:

1. Recognition is more an individual matter and a result of a consideration based on activity over a longer period (less conflicts between innovators on who contributed with what).
2. Organizations are more used to these types of reward systems through leadership and often technical/expert promotion systems as well.
3. Although the promotional system can be systematic and predictable, the released rewards can be adapted to the individual and be more fit-for-purpose.
4. The system can come in addition to other promotional systems, which means for example that a Vice President can also be a Senior Innovator.
5. The reward system can be transparent and predictable.

Incentive systems for Idea Receivers

Innovation gets more and more challenging from top and down in Figure 36. To get an idea can be fairly easy – it happens all the time. To mature it enough to propose it, is a bit harder, but not complicated. To have it accepted by an authority with the power to execute is much harder. Then at least one, but normally many Idea Receivers need to be convinced. And then, to implement, a high number of Passive Users need to be convinced, and that is the real hard part. Increasing complexity top down in Figure 36 is far from a law of nature and there are probably many exceptions, but very often you'll find that this is the case. The best would be that the incentive systems reflect and compensate for these differences. I would, however, claim that to find efficient, fair and reasonable incentive systems is also increasingly difficult top down in Figure 36.

Now to the Idea Receivers –they also need efficient incentive systems to balance out inconveniences with something that motivates. Idea Receivers could be close colleagues, line managers, middle management generally, advisors and specialists, plant and asset managers and leadership, everyone who gets an idea on their table and needs to decide whether or not to actively support it. Most of these groups are often measured on delivering on a pre-planned set of milestones within time and budgets associated to activities within their responsibility area. To get most out of these resources, the plans are ambitious and budgets are tight. This is probably the single largest barrier for innovation around; potential receivers being measured on delivering on a pre-defined plan. Indirectly this means that innovative suggestions are noise and distractions unless they accidently fit within a narrow band, giving the same or better result than something on the plan, faster with less risk (and then not-invented-here kicks inn). Before introducing positive incentives for Idea Receivers, they need first and foremost the barriers removed; flexibility in their objectives to fit in new things easily. Secondly, they need to be measured on their innovation contribution – having KPI's on innovation. Let us exemplify this: It is not unusual in performance reviews and reports that deliveries are colored green, yellow or red to facilitate quick overview of status (greens are OK, yellows alerts and reds out of plan). A simple measure to lift innovative activities, particularly radical, where the tendency otherwise is to end up red on risk, budget and time, is to apply a different color set to those projects. If innovation is sought, these colors would enhance the total impression on the contrary to that dreadful red color often being the case under these circumstances. Then, of course, the leader who evaluates the now so colorful performance document needs to recognize the innovation colors to help create the desire to get more of those innovation type projects into the portfolio. But not too many – also here there must be a sound balance.

Beyond the above, recognizing and promoting innovation is a management and leadership task, so normal management and leadership incentives should be sufficient. However, when management and leadership are evaluated, they should be rewarded not only for delivering on those pre-planned milestones, but also on picking up new innovative possibilities on the way.

Incentive systems for the Passive Users

Incentive systems for Passive Users do necessarily have to be of a different nature than for the two other groups. On the contrary to Idea Proposers and Idea Receivers, the passive users are normally a larger collective crowd, which therefore cannot easily be incentivized individually. An as the name implies, they remain passive for the most.

A common effective incentive we see for this group time and time again is fear for jobs and competitors. We often see a positive effect on innovation when a department, a company or a whole industry gets into a critical situation. It can certainly be discussed how sustainable the positive effect of such negative incentives can be. Often the positive effect disappears with the critical situation, so it seems negative incentives can have a positive effect in the crisis, but less effect in the longer term (the cultural aspect). For example, the innovation pace increased significantly during second world war, but dropped again quickly afterwards.

Positive incentives have a tendency to work better in a long-term, and as such also lift the innovation culture at the same time (see *Building a sustainable innovation culture for growth* on page 182). Positive collective incentives for a large group of innovation users can be linked to early and open information and possibly even involvement.

Open and early information in this context is not only about openly and honestly sharing the reasons why innovation is necessary, but also sharing possible concepts and ideas openly with everyone at an early stage. For this group an early idea implementable a long time from now is less threatening than a decision out of the blue to implement a totally new system tomorrow. With openness at an early idea stage, everyone will see that progress is a question of hard systematic work over a longer period with major changes to the original sketch. Knowledge about this effect takes away some of the fear for details in the early sketch and allows a slow mental maturation on a collective level to the changes that will or at least may come. This type of openness can specifically be articles about ideas and concepts, open online innovation process, hallway expositions, open workshops or leadership focus in speeches and/or town halls.

In addition, if the Passive Users can be involved in idea development somehow, this can be a significant incentive for all parties. Such involvement would turn the development in the direction of open innovation on an internal level. Not only would this improve the flow of ideas that can lift the concept to new heights, but it would also positively address the ever so famous "not-invented-here" syndrome. Collective engagement will prepare the ground for implementation and can potentially lift improvements, which otherwise would fail catastrophically. This type of involvement can be open idea sessions (physical or net-based submissions), idea boxes next to hallway expositions, online voting, or campaigns of different types like crowdsourcing. Involvement can have a tremendous effect. But openness can be a contradiction to investors fearful of radical innovation, and to protection of intellectual property.

Anyway, the incentives discussed above could easily classify as innovation culture builders rather than specific incentives – which is the subject of the next paragraph.

Building a sustainable innovation culture for growth

The ultimate objective for this book and really for any company or group is to create a strong sustainable innovation culture – an active agility allowing the company to stay in the forefront of development, lead the way and create value and meaning not only for the company but making the world a better place too.

Organizational culture can be defined in many ways. Frequently terms like values and behavior linked to social and psychological environment are used to define cultures in organizations. This is not the place to discuss the definition. For this purpose, it is enough to imagine what it takes to build a sustainable organizational identity lasting beyond time-limited campaigns, trends and cycles.

Let us look at how an innovation culture could materialize for the three different groups in Figure 36. Similar to incentives, culture building also becomes increasingly complicated top down in the figure. Let us start at the top:

Building an innovative culture amongst the Idea Proposers

In a strong innovative culture Idea Proposers would typically:

- Focus on possibilities without worrying about what could go wrong on the way
- Hunger for new challenges and business needs whether being told or analytically finding them uninvitedly
- Have half of the brain thinking about new solutions whenever a challenge is brought up in any context
- Consciously and subconsciously notice and remember smart solutions from other contexts, and bring them up when a new challenge is to be solved
- Construct solutions (mentally or documented) to known or imaginative challenges ready to be shared at the right moment
- Ready to share ideas with others confident that this will lift the idea even higher, always after the great feeling of an upwards synergy spiral

- Have the "What if it works" attitude rather than "What could fail" in the idea phase (see Figure 37)
- Test-fast-&-cheap oriented, not worrying about failure as they bring new knowledge and the opportunity to adjust to an even better direction
- Team-oriented and not interested in who came up with what and when in the final concept
- Work visually – thinking, storing and sharing ideas visually in the form of sketches, drawings, models etc.

To build this culture for idea proposers, the following steps should be considered:

- Make sure idea proposals are processed properly including a fair evaluation stating the reason for a possible refusal
    - think user experience – remember that every proposer has many friends he or she will share his or her impression with, spreading both a good and a bad experience very fast in the organization (see more in *Building an innovative culture amongst the Idea Receivers* on page 184)
- Try to introduce an effective incentive system adapted to the current culture in the company (see previous paragraph)
- Lift up not only successful innovations but also associated innovators into the public domain, which

    - is a recognition to the inventors
    - moves innovation closer to everyone by linking innovative success to people familiar from daily work
    - gives focus to innovation at an early stage which can make later implementation easier (the maturing factor is important in innovation)
    - increases exposure of new concepts which again increases the possibility of feed-back, potential improvements, and even customers

- Communicate and appreciate also failed innovations and tests to recognize that failures are an inevitable side effect of success. You cannot have one without the other – lifting up both is therefore essential.

Building an innovative culture amongst the Idea Receivers

A strong innovative culture amongst the Idea Receivers is based on a clear understanding of the connection between maturity and critical mindset (see Figure 37), which indeed can be challenging.

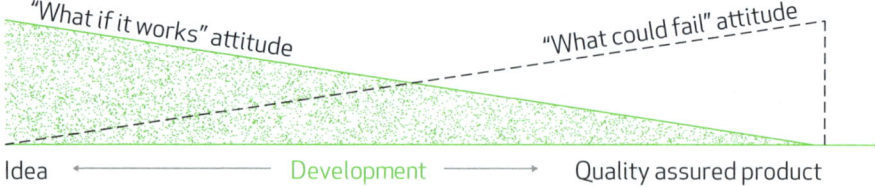

Figure 37   The relation between maturity and critical mindset: When an idea is immature, the focus should be on the possibilities this idea could bring about. Towards the end of the development, when the idea has matured significantly, all stones needs to be turned to reveal weaknesses.

It is perhaps in human nature to be critical to new suggestions one has not come up with or been involved in oneself. In addition to this human-nature factor, many Idea Receivers spend their entire day working in the right side of Figure 37 with soon-to-be-finished implementations, being generally critical and searching for those last risk points to mitigate. Let's say an idea proposer wants to advance the new concept. To advance an associated formal "*Gate Keeper*" needs to be convinced, which turns this person into an Idea Receiver. A Gate Keeper's role is to quality assure what passes the gate, which naturally promotes the "what could go wrong" attitude. This is particularly the case for experts and specialists associated with final quality assurance (QA), who can easily be called in to QA new ideas too. In this situation, unless you are trained to and make particular efforts, the likelihood is that you will approach the new idea proposed (left side of Figure 37) with a critical risk-based mindset too. It may even be too much to ask people totally occupied with QA type of work the entire day to suddenly switch a few minutes and build curiosity and appreciation over a vague possibility between lots of risks. But in order to progress, this is detrimental. Anyone can stop any new immature idea, no matter how good, by searching for risk points. No particular skills needed. The problem is to find the valuable possibilities well hidden in between the less valuable possibilities and swarmed over by risk. This is what takes skills. To accomplish this, as a minimum, Idea Receivers need to understand and master the left side of Figure 37, and know in day-to-day situations which side to apply (see also innovation leadership theory in *Shepherd leadership and framing the search* on page 85).

A quick way to start building a process where the left side of Figure 37 is respected is to make sure that Idea Receivers, at least the formal Idea Receivers, must have been Idea Proposers at least once. With experience from the other side of the table, as an Idea Proposer, the likelihood is that the Idea Receiver will consciously or subconsciously know the importance of the Figure 37 attitude. He or she would also have a better understanding of how the world appears from a proposer viewpoint and would be in a better position to give a positive impression, whether the proposed idea is accepted or not, the importance of which we will discuss below.

So, it takes more than just mastering the left side of Figure 37. In a strong innovative culture Idea Receivers would typically

- Take idea proposals seriously, but this does not mean that all ideas are to be accepted for further maturation
- Be curious
- Log all proposals systematically (perhaps using an ERP system, see More about under *Incentive systems for the Idea Proposers* page 174)
- Think testing quick and cheap, as opposed to direct answers based on "gut feelings". Perhaps the Idea Receiver can get surprised too – history is full of people who thought they knew, but were diametrically wrong.
    ◦ Invest a minimum amount of resources in each idea to perform the test

- Let the Idea Proposer perform the test – if it fails, as will often be the case, it is ALWAYS better that the proposer informs the receiver about this rather than the opposite. The likelihood is that the proposer will learn from a test failure and come back with improved proposals

- If a refusal is necessary, give a thorough reason for the refusal
- In the case of accepted ideas, the Idea Receiver takes active ownership of the idea and actively tries to promote the idea. The more active supporters an idea has, the higher probability for success.

  - Join the network of the proposer(s) and earlier receivers, and merge it with your own network
  - Help look for the ultimate receiver; internal customers who are willing to pay for development

- Knows that everyone's first idea is special and needs special attention.

The following perspective is useful to keep in mind when designing a system for receiving ideas: All Idea Proposers have many friends and close colleagues. The Idea Proposer's impression after bringing forward a proposal, whether the result is positive or negative, will be spoken about around the coffee machine and at lunch. Their impression will travel with the "speed of light" through the company. Therefore, a positive overall impression, whether the outcome for the idea was positive or negative, is vital to develop innovation culture – but then it will be an effective contributor.

Below (Figure 38) are examples of how an Idea Receiver could answer when a colleague comes into his/her office and proudly presents an idea he or she has come up with. A common metaphor is to have an angel on one shoulder and devil in the other, whispering things in your ears – and you are not sure whom to listen to.

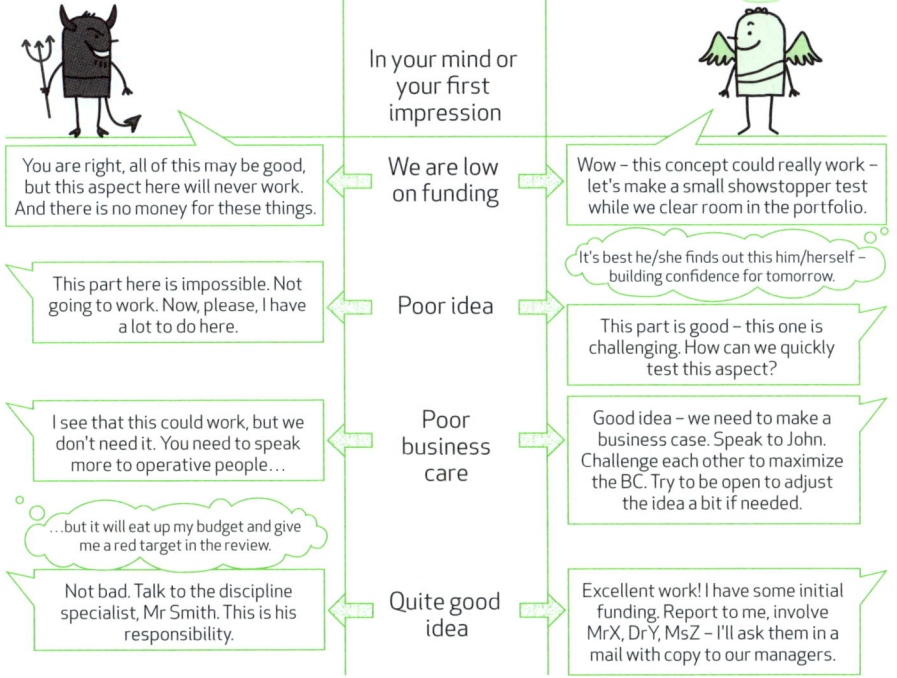

Figure 38 Dialogue examples when someone reporting to you comes into your office with a suggestion. The way you choose to answer may be very decisive not only for how this particular idea will develop but also for how your colleague will act in the future.

But in practical terms, receiving ideas takes more than one short sentence like those illustrated in Figure 38. It is about climbing a ladder together with the idea proposer, where each step represents one accomplishment, and requires some sort of recognition. These steps are listed here:

1. Develop an idea
2. Come forward and propose the idea
3. Address a real business need
4. Any element in contradiction with physics or any other clear showstopper
5. A positive business case
6. A realistic execution system

I have proposed a high number of ideas over the years and the vast majority of receivers jump straight to Step 6, which is about evaluating details, then find a weak point and consequently choose to take on an expressed negative attitude to the proposal. This is an excellent way to stop ideas, to make sure that you will have less ideas brought to your attention in the future and to counterwork innovation culture building. The rest of us who really want innovation and progress should consider the other points in chronological order and postpone the last step until the time is right. Perhaps it could help to think about each individual's desire to innovate as a bank account, to which people around them can make deposits and withdrawals. Recognizing the real efforts made makes deposits. Failing to do so is withdrawals. Deposits and withdrawals can be made irrespective of the outcome of the idea itself (whether the idea is accepted or not).

So, let us go back to the imaginary person in our office proposing a new idea. *Step 1 and 2* (see the list above) can be recognized immediately, even before the idea is communicated. The easiest way is simply to express something in the following direction: "On behalf of the company I would like to express gratitude not only for taking the effort to create a new idea and therefore also a potential opportunity for our company, but also to have the courage to come forward with it." You can also add: "I am, in fact, honored that you show me the confidence to come here and share it." These sentences state clearly that you recognize there is an effort behind an idea, that is takes courage to propose something believed to be new in the sense that no one else has thought about this before, and that you understand that ideas are sensitive and not necessarily shared with everyone. However, you also get to say that the company takes ideas seriously and appreciates such contributions. Your next step of progress on a personal level will be not only to *say* these things, but also genuinely *mean* them when you say it.

I have also come across idea receivers who fail to share the enthusiasm they in fact have for an idea, as if this situation is a state of negotiation, where revealing interest or even enthusiasm could weaken the receiver's side when the "deal will land". This behavior would then typically play out as listening suspiciously with a "poker face" when the idea is being presented and then perhaps point at someone else to consult further without any additional feedback of significance. In certain cases, I have met these people coincidentally at a later stage where they have asked for idea status expressing how useful it would have been to have the idea realized. This is failing to recognize Step 1 and 2, and if the "bank account" was low before this meeting, it could mean the end of the idea right there and then.

Step 3 is the first consideration after seeing and understanding the idea. The question in Step 3 is whether or not the idea is addressing a present or future business need for the company? This question addresses the framing issue we have spoken about before (see under the heading *Shepherd leadership* on page 85): Is the idea within a frame the company would like to be explored or not? If the idea fails here, it may still be a good idea, but it would be outside the company's scope and should be stopped internally. If, however, it does not fail and the idea appears to be within scope, make sure to recognize that too. For an immature idea this may well be enough to continue. In practical terms, this means that another person or team is trying to map unknown territory interesting to the company. At an early stage the cost is (normally) very limited and the learning curve quite steep, so even if the idea in its present state seems poor, this may well develop into something interesting. Try to keep the search on a simple level, in which case the risk and cost remain low and you assure more eyes on a potentially valuable field of development.

At this point it could be useful to divide feedback into two categories:

1. Considerations to base a possible decision on whether or not to spend company resources continuing to work on the idea (like Step 3)
2. Information and insight that may become useful for the Idea Proposer in the development work ahead

Step 4 is about considering whether or not the idea is aligned with or up against physics and laws of nature. Some will put this step into Category 1 and use this to judge whether to stop the idea or not. This is to an extent understandable, because the laws of nature are hard to beat and resources are always limited. But I can also understand those who would put Step 4 into Category 2. Although laws of nature are hard to challenge, there is also the possibility to turn this the other way around and introduce changes that will adapt the concept to the laws of nature. The intellectual efforts a motivated person can mobilize using ownership of an idea with an improvement potential are almost endless. Therefore, as long as Step 3 is met, the limits of physics can generate very useful insights, which again can bring the concept just onto the feasible side of these limits. And it will most certainly create a learning experience.

Step 5 is focusing on the economic sides of the concept and how the invention will create value. Like Step 4, feedback on this step can be put in both Category 1 and 2, although probably leaning more towards Category 2 than Step 4 did. The same arguments apply. Early phase ideas have a steep learning curve for low effort and cost. A business model will change over time and should not be emphasized too much at an early stage. It took the tractor decades to become competitive with the horse. Demanding a positive business case during the first years would have killed the tractor project. However, radical concepts also need a cost benefit consideration, but one should not forget the value of exploring new territory by especially motivated individuals and understand that a business case can be highly dynamic at this level (one day low, the next day adventurously high). While incremental projects need a positive business case as presented, radical concepts need a positive business case in the future for which they are meant.

Step 6 points to the way a concept will be realized and will therefore be about details connected to execution. I have seen quite a few ideas in my time and I cannot remember a single one where the details in the original "first thought" have not changed as the idea has matured. Therefore, it is close to pointless to look at this information in Category 1, as basis for a go/no-go decision. It is almost at the limit to bring Step 6 into Category 2 (as useful information for the Idea Proposer) during an early stage since this will change anyway. However, insight can always be useful. Just make sure this insight is clearly communicated as loose thoughts that may or may not be taken into account at an early stage.

However, I often experience that many Idea Receivers skip feedback on Step 1 through 5, and jump straight to Step 6, on which they base their support considerations (Category 1). Idea Receivers need training and preferably also innovation experience to handle their important function well.

The long-term consequences may be larger than a conversation between two people.

Before jumping to the next subject, it could be useful to comment on the classic "we have tried this before and it didn't work" answer to a hopeful inventor. Step 1 and 2 has obviously been fulfilled as this response came about in the first place. The likelihood of Step 3 being fulfilled too, (that there exists a need for the proposed solution) is certainly there since the issue being communicated has been on the agenda before. The next consideration is about basic physics and major showstoppers. If the suggestion doesn't meet these requirements, I would suggest that feedback should be about physics and showstoppers, and not that the concept has been tried before. So now we are down to Step 5 and 6, which is more Category 2 feedback then Category 1. The fact that concepts have been on the table before is absolutely not a good reason to stop things again. If the reason for stopping this in the first place was a rational thing to do (which certainly may not have been the case), so many circumstances around the concept may have changed in our dynamic world since previous proposal. In addition, aspects of the new idea may be different too, in total creating new possibilities. Besides, reference to earlier attempts failing rarely satisfies an eager inventor. Earlier experience with new proposals may be beneficial to the idea receiver since this may be a good source of information if documentation or knowledge are still available, but the basis for feedback should be about the idea at hand as concretely as possible. A clever receiver could, however, use historical knowledge to connect people with similar ideas in order to spark yet a higher level of solutions.

Building an innovative culture amongst the Passive Users

The most difficult part is to build a sustainable and strong innovation culture amongst the Passive Users – the rest of the company. I am afraid there are no quick fixes here. This takes targeted systematic and hard work over a longer period. Central elements in this hard work could be:

- Start the culture work from the top of Figure 36 and work downwards (or said in a different way, follow the recipe in this book). Generating momentum amongst the Idea Proposers, and later Idea Receivers, will have a positive effect on the Passive User group. However, this is a steep uphill pull in the beginning, since the Passive Users will have a negative influence on innovation flow.

- Communicate the need for change and progress in an open and honest manner. Shortcuts here will be counterproductive when (not if) the truth surfaces.
- Communicate innovation success stories and honor those who deserves honoring. Let real faces and real people shine in glory to make the distance from the successful innovators to the general Passive User as short as possible.

  ◦ This is one of the important reasons for building innovation capacity internally as opposed to subcontracting or buying the effort externally – the distance to the Passive Users increases and implementation as well as culture building suffer.

- Create an effective incentive system for Idea Proposers and Idea Receivers (see previous paragraph) for a general innovation pace increase.
- Involve the Passive Users as much as possible in the ongoing innovation effort in the company (see more details in *Incentive systems for the Passive Users* on page 180).
- Communicate business needs to which Passive Users can propose solutions (to become an Idea Proposer).
- Then, create a clear idea submission point where ideas can formally be proposed, and a proper process which will:

  ◦ give each idea a fair chance
  ◦ lift the best idea all the way
  ◦ communicate refusals properly with a stated reason (remembering that each proposer has at least ten friends with whom they will share the overall impression).

This will slowly but steadily lift the overall innovation culture in the company. This will take time. There may not be too many things one can do to effectively speed up the process. There is, however, one thing that can make the speed less slow (but still not fast) and this is to understand and apply the Iceberg Principle of Leadership.

The Iceberg Principle of Leadership

Within innovation it is important to mobilize positive effort and enthusiasm amongst those involved in innovation. This is as valid for the ideation phase via the implementation phase through the use of the invention, which means it is as important for Idea Proposers and Idea Receivers as it is for the Passive Users. The Iceberg Principle of Leadership[12] in an innovation context is about mobilizing full, positive effort in everyone involved.

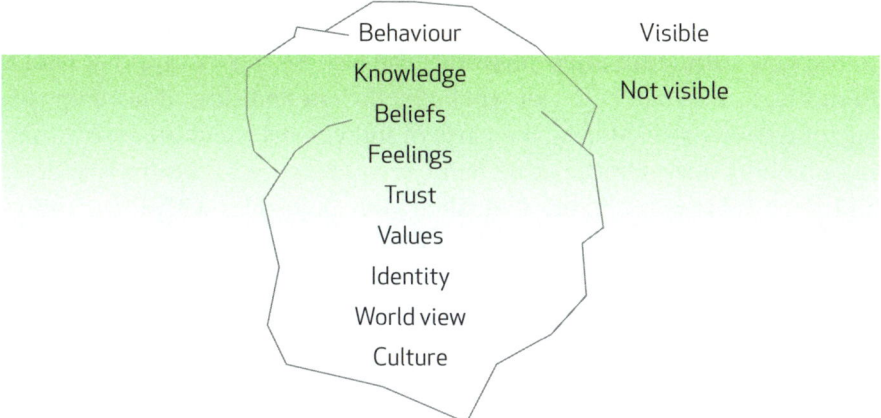

Figure 40   The Iceberg theory of Leadership: We see people's behavior, but we do not see their softer sides like Culture and Values. We will significantly increase individuals' full positive effort if our objectives are well aligned with all the invisible soft sides, and the effect on the project or the organization can be tremendous.

The core of the Iceberg Principle of Leadership is related to one of the most known characteristics of an Iceberg – the fact that only a small fraction of the total volume is visible above water, or said in a different way; the by far largest part and arguably the most important part of the iceberg is not visible from the surface, a well-known and feared fact for those traveling Arctic and Antarctic near oceans (see Figure 40). The Iceberg Principle of Leadership alludes to the same principle in human beings. There is the part of people around us we can see, and there is the part of them we cannot see, the latter being the most important part to unlock with respect to positive effort and enthusiasm. The part we can see, things like gender, skin color, general appearance and behavior, are not particularly suited to reveal who we really are. Who we really are can be found in the much larger and far more important part of us others cannot see. These are the inner parts of us, like knowledge, experience, values, convictions, sense of worth, feelings, identity, culture and world view.

In a company context and particularly in a culture change discussion of the things we see, the behavior is our focal point. And we would like to make people change parts of their behavior, adapt to and even contribute to the new culture we are promoting. The iceberg theory says that efforts to motivate a certain behavior will be inefficient and slow, if not impossible, unless you also address the parts of individuals we do not see – their invisible soft sides. On the other hand, if you manage to positively address all the invisible parts mentioned, align your objectives with those things that really make up who we are, the momentum and energy impact can be tremendous. In our metaphor with the iceberg, you can just imagine which direction the iceberg would take of the wind blows one way on the visible part above the sea line, while the sea current acts the opposite direction on the large part below the sea line. The more your company's objectives (or project objectives) are aligned with people's inner sense of being, the faster this change can occur.

You know you have an excellent innovation culture if everyone has been in all three categories in Figure 36.

Good luck in your innovation work!

Appendix A: Academic perspective by Dr. Ingunn Johanne Ness

Quite soon after we started our Equinor radical innovation pilot group back in 2011, we had the pleasure to have Dr. Ingunn Johanne Ness following our group regularly over a 2-year period as one of three similar types of innovation groups as a basis for her Ph.D. work. For more about Ingunn, see the summary in the end of this appendix. During the course of her Ph.D. work, she observed and analyzed our behavior, interviewed our contributors and wrote her thesis on findings from all three groups. I challenged Ingunn, who holds a unique and unfiltered external perspective on our work, to share with the readers of this book some of the insights she acquired during her interactions with our radical innovation group. Here is what she wrote:

The Equinor radical innovation pilot group – a case in a Ph.D. project on interdisciplinary innovation work

When I was a Ph.D. candidate at the University of Bergen, Faculty of Psychology, Department of Education, I had the Equinor radical innovation pilot group as one of three cases in my project[20]. It was a true privilege to explore creative processes in interdisciplinary groups and I saw how deep and advanced expert knowledge from different practices in a group can ignite imagination.

Choosing the Equinor radical innovation pilot group as a case

In my search for interesting cases to study in different knowledge intensive organizations, I contacted Equinor and was happy to find this particular group since they met the criteria that I felt were important: *gathering people from different disciplines with an aim to develop innovative ideas.*

I was excited to get access to authentic innovation work and to be able to follow (among two other groups) Steinar's group once a week over almost a 2-year period. To me it was important to be there, in the group with the rest of the group members and in the mist of where it all happened. I wanted to unravel some of the mystery around creative processes and how interdisciplinary groups best can make magic happen – because true innovation does not happen automatically – we need to understand what the processes look like when they are successful. As many of us already have experienced, interdisciplinary group work can be challenging and when the aim is to develop something new together, it is even more difficult. This aim was also shared by Steinar, as leader of the group – and he talked about his visions in enthusiastic ways.

Collecting data in the Equinor radical innovation pilot group

Creativity as a collective phenomenon needs to be investigated closely – in particular as the time has come to stop thinking "in silos" and to start collaborating across disciplinary boundaries. The pilot group was created exactly with this purpose.

In order to study the creative processes, it was important to spend time in the groups in order to see first-hand how the processes developed. In a way I sought to become almost like an ordinary member and investigate how specialists from different disciplines developed innovative ideas in collaboration. (For further reading, see[22]). I was particularly interested in the interaction and the communication in the groups and which patterns I could identify. Said in another way: I wanted to open up the "black box" and describe what really happens when a group actually develops something new and innovative. In order to "find the recipe", I needed to experience the group work and observe ideas develop from beginning to end. So, I followed their meetings every Monday. In addition to taking notes, I brought an audio recorder and made recordings of the conversations in all the groups. I also video recorded some of the sessions. After each observation, I immediately started transcribing the same day when the interactions were still "fresh" in my mind. This was a lot of work – to write down everything that had been said and by whom – but very important in order to follow the different ideas over a period of time.

In addition to observations, I conducted both group interviews and interviews with the group leaders. The leader interviews helped me to gain a deeper understanding of the role of the leaders and how they reflected on the creative processes. I found interviewing the leaders of innovation processes in organizations very useful. I asked them questions regarding the specific work that was conducted in the groups, and also questions about their leadership vision as well as questions regarding how they saw organizational structure influencing innovation work.

As the project developed and I collected a lot of data, I felt an enormous responsibility in how I processed and stored the sensitive data. It would be very unfortunate, to say the least, if sensitive information was revealed through my research and reached competing organizations. Therefore, I had to be very careful in how I both stored and used the data. Interestingly, this extreme business sensitivity proved later to be a challenge when it came to reporting and using quotes to help demonstrate how the innovative ideas were developed.

Findings – the creative processes developing through six phases

So – what did I find? What patterns could I identify that described the creative processes, not only in the Equinor radical innovation pilot group but across all the groups I studied?

During the initial analyses of the data I was reading the transcripts searching for ideas ending in an innovative result, so that I could track them back and see how they had actually developed.

In this way I discovered that the groups' communication patterns and interactions changed over time. At one point the communication was more open, more questions, more creative and imaginative, while other times it seemed as if the communication were more "closed" and not as explorative. As I studied the patterns involved, I found that creative processes seemed to develop throughout six phases of initial innovation work[24].

In phase one, the group members were assembled for the first time and informed about the task by the group leaders. This also included how the leaders wanted the group members to collaborate with each other – given the fact that they came from different disciplines and had different expertise.

They were provided with a challenge or a "need" to work on and the innovative group work could begin. I called this phase, the "Initiation phase".

After this initial phase, group members started to give presentations and share their individual knowledge related to the task at hand. This generally included sharing discipline-related specific terminologies and it was obvious that the different group members saw matters from very different perspectives and had distributed knowledge, so I called this phase the "Knowledge distribution phase." However, it is also challenging when people use different terminologies and it can be hard to understand each other.

A profession, an institution or a department, develops its own social language. This is why group members from different departments, used different concepts and terms. Still, if group members were to succeed in building on each other's ideas and combine them, they had to make themselves understood. When the group members formulated their expert views during discussions, it was noticeable how they experimented with words and concepts that enabled them to convey meaning for themselves as well as for the others. Svein (anonymous group member) in the innovation pilot group commented this meaning making process like this:

It is interesting how we have to also understand our own knowledge on another level and form than we normally do when we use the "tribal language" within our own discipline, when we must communicate our knowledge to others.

Then, when they had shared knowledge in this rather calm and structured way, they started to discuss what they had just shared. Clearly, they disagreed based on their different perspectives and different ways of understanding or communicating matters, so consequently they started to challenge each other's standpoints and views in loud and lively discussions. The many voices blended together, and it seemed as if they were participating on equal terms and that no voice was superior to the others. I thus called this the "Polyphony phase" from the musical term. In this phase the group members across the groups also seemed to be quite eager and engaged and really discussed the matter at hand.

One example is when Svein has described the functions of a particular system to the rest of the group. Steinar does not agree and challenges Svein:

Steinar: But I would not agree. I would claim that you need to remove the (…).
Svein: But then you will get a more passive system.
Steinar: Ok, I understand – but I still believe that, even though I might not know too much about this particular detail, if you have this (…), then it will become incompatible with this (…). Is that so?
Svein: No, because it is possible to use the particular (…) in some cases.
Steinar: Ok, so that means that everything which is within this (…), will give in – which again means that this (…) works like this.

Due to the confidentiality agreement, I cannot reveal what they were developing and discussing, but what we see is a typical example of how the group members seemed eager to understand each other, at the same time as they also were eager to state their opinions. Consequently, there was now more tension in the communication compared to the previous phases. Friction was at its most explicit in this phase (for more, see[24]).

After the group members had been discussing various views, they seemed to start using this shared knowledge in new ways and discussed possible new scenarios and imagined new ways to understand or solve the task at hand. Therefore, I called this phase the "Imagination phase."

The following is an example of how the radical innovation pilot group worked in the Imagination phase. The group members had been sitting around a table, discussing a subject and they were now in the phase where they began to use the shared knowledge in imagining new ways of doing things and moved to draw on the smart board.

This is an excerpt from a field observation: *The group leader gets up from his chair and starts to draw circles on the smart board. His voice is eager and engaged. Another group member fills in some details and quickly makes room for another group member who indicates that he wants to add something. They are all standing shoulder-to-shoulder in front of the smart board, all intensely focusing on the drawings. Soon the circles are filled with details representing their individual inputs and ideas, but now visualized as one common drawing.*

These scenarios and new views became increasingly formulated into concrete ideas, in what I called the "Idea formulation phase", before they finally were combined into the last "Consolidation phase" and could be presented as an innovative idea, solution or business case.

When I looked closer at these six phases, I noticed that in the three first phases (initiation, knowledge distribution, and polyphony) the group members seemed to share knowledge and learn from each other. In this way they built a common knowledge platform, which was crucial in the actual idea development that took place in the three last phases (imagination, idea formulation, consolidation). It seemed that the more they learned from each other, the more innovative ideas seemed to be developed. Then again, if the distance was too far between their perspectives, the communication broke down. A certain overlap was necessary in order to ensure progression. Further, I found that the first phases could be seen as input, and the concrete ideas and results as output, and that the most creative part happened in the three middle phases. In the polyphony, imagination, and idea formulation phases, group members challenged each other's views, they disagreed and negotiated in a circular movement – and pushed the limits of existing knowledge. Thus, I coined these phases as the "Room of Opportunity." In this "room", group members co-constructed new ideas and it was clear that the tension stimulated new ideas.

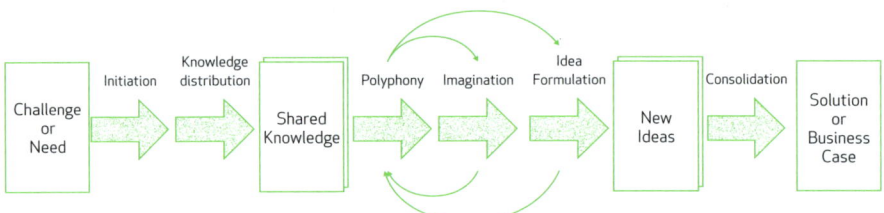

Figure 41 The Room of Opportunity[22]

However, it is important to know that in creativity research literature there has been some rather negative findings on the group idea-sharing process and that people often have conflicts or become too conforming in groups.

On the other hand, Paulus and his colleagues [19, 25] suggested that sharing of ideas in groups would trigger more associations or ideas. Idea sharing individuals in groups are exposed to more ideas during their session than individuals generating ideas on their own. In other words, there is a lot of potential for cognitive stimulation in groups, if the group members attend carefully to the shared ideas [26, p. 77]. In the Equinor radical innovation pilot group with interdisciplinary members, they managed to keep a respectful tone even during heated discussions and disagreements – also due to how Steinar facilitated the meetings with humor and enthusiasm.

Underlying conditions for succeeding

Since it was obvious that one of the keys to developing innovative ideas was that the different disciplines in the groups could learn from each other, I narrowed the focus to look at how knowledge and ideas were built across boundaries between different disciplines and what underlying conditions were needed for this to happen.

Findings showed that it was necessary for group members from different disciplines to have the ability to recognize and acknowledge others' competence as resources and not as a threat to their own expertise. Despite the fact that at this stage in the process there was an urge to challenge each other's views openly, this was done in a respectful manner.

In order to construct a foundation for developing ideas, the negotiation of perspectives seemed to imply friction and some disagreement across all groups. To succeed with the innovation work, it seemed crucial that the group members saw each other as resources. Three underlying conditions were identified: openness (that people in the groups show interest in each other and are open to other suggestions and ways of seeing the world), curiosity (that they ask questions and want to find out and understand what the others think), and respect (that they accept different opinions and show politeness even when they disagree the most). (For more, see[23]).

An example that shows how group members seem open and curious towards each other is the following made by Steinar:

Steinar (radical innovation pilot group): *I am really curious, I am… because when you said this, Miriam, I get "goose bumps" – it is so exciting to me, I am eager, you have all this "prima" knowledge on this so can you tell me how the (…) can be attached to (…)?* He laughs and gives Miriam a big smile.

I interpreted this quote as Steinar being both curious and interested in Miriam's knowledge and what she had to say. He stated that he got "goose bumps" and he smiled and showed eagerness, interest and expressed the fact that he wanted to learn more.

My results in other groups also showed that it is not simply adequate to merely bring together group members from different disciplines, but that successful innovative groups require an awareness of the processes and relational competencies in order for the collaboration and learning to succeed.

The leaders stimulated imagination and the development of innovative ideas by paying attention to diversity in experiences and knowledge and also by encouraging various roles among the group members. For more, see for instance[21].

Reflecting on my time in the Equinor radical innovation pilot group – and looking towards the future

Organizational creativity is a precondition of innovation. Consequently, organizational creativity is a field that is becoming more and more important in organizations aiming to survive and thrive in our complex knowledge society.

My Ph.D. research focused on investigating the creative processes in interdisciplinary groups working with developing innovative ideas. I also wanted to understand the relational processes and the social interaction. As a senior researcher on this topic, I spend time discussing innovation with both national and international colleagues and travel to conferences all over the world. One thing seems to be a common hinderance across countries – too often we only evaluate the product and do not pay enough consideration to the processes. The Equinor radical innovation pilot group, however, paid attention to the processes and was a great case. I think this is a way for

Equinor to create a more innovative culture in the whole organization: to take a systematic approach to the creative processes leading to innovation.

As previously stated, the time has come to stop thinking "in silos" and to start collaborating across disciplinary boundaries. The pilot group had exactly this purpose. Even though the group met for only 2.5 hours a week, this was still enough to create results because the meetings happened every week – there was continuation. In this way the group members also got to know each other. Creative work in interdisciplinary settings involves leaving one's comfort zone and the risk of sharing "silly ideas" or asking "silly questions" when facing unfamiliar expertise. But it can be that exact "silly question" that opens up a new way of thinking, which might lead to something radically new. Therefore, it is important to pay attention to the climate in the group and that leaders of such processes contribute to a safe climate that encourages people to "dive in" and actively participate. It is not enough to gather group members with top specialized competency, the group work needs to be facilitated and the group needs to be functioning in order to be successful. Steinar was aware if this – and his enthusiasm and good mood helped everybody to relax and have fun. When observing and talking with Steinar, it became clear early on that he had high ambitions for his group and Equinor as a company. In addition, I experienced that he was also interested in my thoughts and ideas after each session. We discussed what had worked and what had been less useful. Often traditional brain storming sessions skip the discussions and co-construction of ideas – they move too quickly from challenge to solution. If a radical idea is the goal, then it is important to spend enough time exploring. I believe that the radical innovation pilot group worked well in that sense.

To me it was very interesting to follow different groups but I spent the most time in the radical innovation pilot group – this was due to the fact that they had frequent meetings so that it was possible to keep a close track on the different ideas on which they were working. During my time in the group, I presented what I had found to Equinor and the group. It was important to give something back to Equinor for giving me access to real innovation processes – and I do believe that Steinar also felt our conversations were interesting and useful for him and that my project would bring important and useful knowledge to Equinor. After all, understanding how to succeed with interdisciplinary innovation work, is quite timely for both Equinor and our society. I think that this way of working in an organization such as Equinor, is crucial in order to meet the future.

My suggestion would be to set up several radical innovation groups all over the company and to educate, offer courses, and train employees in systematic innovation methods like this book offers. In addition, I would recommend that the courses include a key to succeeding: competency in how to work in interdisciplinary teams. We are facing global changes and serious challenges – these require creativity and sustainable, interdisciplinary solutions.

I am looking forward to following Equinor into the future.

About Ingunn Johanne Ness

Bio: Dr. Ingunn Johanne Ness is a senior researcher and Cluster Leader at the Centre for the Science of Learning & Technology (SLATE). She has a Ph.D. from the University of Bergen, Faculty of Psychology, Department of Education, and a postdoctoral degree from the Faculty of Psychology, SLATE. Ness leads the innovative research future efforts in SLATE and carries out research on interdisciplinary collaboration, innovation, creativity, and leadership. Ness has a particular interest for the sociocultural approach and works with one of the world's leading environments on sociocultural theory, the OSAT group at the Department of Education, University of Oxford. In addition, Ness has close collaboration with businesses such as Equinor. She has a number of publications in international journals and handbooks and her main teaching areas are creative knowledge processes, innovative methods and supervision of Master and Ph.D. students. Ness is co-editor in a Special Issue in The Creativity Research Journal, Section Editor for the Palgrave Encyclopedia of the Possible, Associate Editor of The European Journal of Psychology and co-editor on dialogical pedagogy, creativity and learning, KLIM publishing, Denmark.

Terms and expressions

Here is a short explanation of some central terms and expressions used in this book. Please note that there exist many different definitions more or less similar. The explanations given here are the associations attached to the corresponding expression throughout this book.

Business need: A need that unlocks business potential and value creation if met.
Innovation: The process of transforming new ideas into real business value.
Incremental innovation: Innovation that builds on the knowledge of the previous version, or in other words, further development of existing products, processes, procedures and/or services.
Radical innovation: Technical innovation that requires new knowledge compared to the previous version, or in other words, breaks out in new direction to existing products, processes, procedures and/or service.
Disruptive innovation: Like radical innovation, but for a business model innovation. New business model makes the knowledge of the business model it replaces obsolete.
Boomerang effect of radical innovation: When you spend time imagining the future in a rather long perspective and use this insight to inspire

those dealing with incremental innovation in order to increase the pace of the incremental development, you apply the Boomerang effect of radical innovation. Note that this inspiration can be built upon quite superficial radical ideas and concepts, long before any realization of these radical ideas.

Dual interdependent innovation: You have accomplished dual interdependency when your radical innovation is positively influencing incremental innovation (the Boomerang effect of radical innovation), but also the other way around, when the increased pace in incremental innovation positively influences your radical efforts.

Ambidexterity: This literally means being two-handed, like if you write as well with your left hand as your right. Within innovation and leadership, this refers to handling incremental and radical innovation differently, with "two hands", acknowledging that these two types of innovation demand different treatments to prosper.

Future scenario: A comprehensive set of innovations, both incremental but particularly radical, making up a complete model of the future within a certain area. Such a future scenario makes it easier to make sound decisions about the future in the present than single concepts taken out of their context.

Continuous improvement: An ongoing permanent improvement process of products, processes, procedures and/or services in order to increase their value. These improvements are normally, but not necessarily of incremental nature.

Alignment leadership: A leadership style with the objective to align people and activities to follow common goals, respect common rules, adhere to common best practice and act predictably in order to maximize output, maintain quality, assure safety and reliability. This is typically the leader style in operative environments with high numbers of products in operative environments with busy production and a high number of people involved.

Framed search: A leadership style often applied in innovative situations where the leader or organizer sets a frame for the innovative search and leaves the participants to search freely within the frame, only to take action if anyone drifts out of the frame.

Showstopper: In the context of innovation a showstopper is a discovery or event which is of such negative significance that it will eliminate confidence in potential success amongst the stakeholders – just or unjust.

Roadmap: A rough or detailed plan to take a project from Situation A, for example now, to Situation B, for example a Future Scenario.

Agile: Agile is a work method or philosophy based on flexibility, effective advancement and quick adaptability to expected or unexpected changes in or around the project.

Multiskill/Interdisciplinary: High variation of skill sets amongst individuals in a group of people, making the collective knowledge and experience base in the group wide and comprehensive.

References

[1] Kahneman, D. (2011). *Thinking, Fast and Slow* (ISBN: 9780141033570). London: Penguin.

[2] Ries, E. (2011). *The Lean Startup* (ISBN: 0307887898). New York: Random House.

[3] Burcharth, A.L.d.A. & Fosfuri, A. (2014). Not invented here: how institutionalized socialization practices affect the formation of negative attitudes toward external knowledge. *Industrial and Corporate Change*. doi:10.1093/icc/dtu018

[4] Martin, R.L. (2011). Fixing the game: bubbles, crashes, and what capitalism can learn from the NFL. *Harvard Business Press*.

[5] O'Reilly III, C.A. & Tushman, M.L. (2004). The ambidextrous organization. *Harvard Business Review, 82*(4), 1–10.

[6] O'Reilly, C.A. & Tushman, M.L. (2011). Organizational ambidexterity: how managers explore and exploit. *California Management Review, 53*(4), 5–22.

[7] Tushman, M.L. & O'Reilly, C.A. (1996). Ambidextrous organizations: managing evolutionary and revolutionary change. *California Management Review, 38*, 8–30.

[8] Tushman, M.L. & O'Reilly, C.A. (2007). Winning through innovation: a practical guide to leading organizational change and renewal. *Harvard Business School Press*.

[9] Tushman, M.L., O'Reilly, C.A. & Harreld, J.B. (2013). *Leading Strategic Renewal: Proactive Punctuated Change through Innovation Streams and Disciplined Learning*.

[10] Spradlin, D. (2012). Are you solving the right problem: most firms aren't, and that undermines performance. *Harvard Business Review*.

[11] Leonard-Barton, D. (1992). Core capabilities and core rigidities: a paradox in managing new product development. *Strategic Management Journal, 13*, 111–125.

[12] Hemingway, E.M. (1959). *The Art of the Short Story*.

[13] Hill, L. & Lineback, K. (2011). *Being the Boss: The 3 Iperatives for Becoming a Great Leader* (ISBN: 9781633692121).

[14] Jostein N.-M. (2015), «Oppvasken» på norsk sokkel kan koste over 500 milliarder. *E24 Dine Penger*. https://e24.no/energi/i/ddWoAo/oppvasken-paa-norsk-sokkel-kan-koste-over-500-milliarder

[15] Hansen, B. & Østerhus, S. (2007). Faroe Bank Channel overflow 1995–2005, *Progress in Oceanography 75*, s. 817–856.

[16] Christensen, C.M. (1997). *The Innovator's Dilemma*. New York: HarperCollins Publishers.

[17] Drucker, P.F. (1985). *Innovation and Entrepreneurship*. New York: Harper Business.

[18] Moore, G.A. (1991). *Crossing the Chasm*. New York: HarperCollins Publishers.

[19] Brown, V.R., Tumeo, M., Larey, T.S. & Paulus, P.B. (1998). Modeling cognitive interactions during group brainstorming. *Small Group Research, 29*(4), 495–526.

[20] Ness, I.J. (2016). *The Room of Opportunity. Understanding How Knowledge and Ideas Are Constructed in Multidisciplinary Groups Working with Innovative Ideas* (Ph.D., Dissertation for the degree of Ph.D.). Bergen: Department of Education, Faculty of Psychology, University of Bergen.

[21] Ness, I.J. (2017). Polyphonic orchestration – facilitating creative knowledge processes for innovation. *European Journal of Innovation Management, 20*(4), 557–577. doi:10.1108/EJIM-05-2016-0049

[22] Ness, I.J. (2019). Behind the scenes: how to research creative processes in multidisciplinary groups. I: I. Lebuda & V.P. Glaveanu (red.), *The Palgrave Handbook of Social Creativity Research* (pp. 353–373). Cham, Switzerland: Palgrave Macmillan.

[23] Ness, I.J. & Riese, H. (2015). Openness, curiosity and respect: underlying conditions

for developing innovative knowledge and ideas between disciplines. *Learning Culture and Social Interaction, 6* (September), 29–39. doi:10.1016/j.lcsi.2015.03.001

[24] Ness, I.J. & Søreide, G.E. (2014). The room of opportunity: understanding phases of creative knowledge processes in innovation. *Journal of Workplace Learning, 26*(8), 545–560. doi:10.1108/JWL-10-2013-0077

[25] Paulus, P.B. (2000). Groups, teams, and creativity: the creative potential of idea-generating groups. *Applied Psychology: An International Review, 49*(2), 237–262.

[26] Paulus, P.B. & Yang, H.-C. (2000). Idea generation in groups: a basis for creativity in organizations. *Organizational Behaviour and Human Decision Processes, 82*(1), 76–87.

[27] Kurzwell, R. (1999). *The Age of Spiritual Machines.* New York: Viking Press.

[28] Google Cloud. *Creating a Culture of Innovation.* https://gsuite.google.co.in/intl/en_in/learn-more/creating_a_culture_of_innovation.html

Index

Symbols
10X method 68, 70

A
acceptance of failure 92, 93
administrative work 45
agility 135
alignment 135
Alignment Leadership 85
ambidexterity 66, 118, 168
ambidextrous 144
ambidextrous leadership 120
aviation industry example 150

B
Boomerang effect 160
build a group 36
building blocks 97
business case 187
business model 122
business need 58, 187

C
cash machine 120
communication 118
communication pattern 199
consolidation 202
continuous improvement 19
core group 46
creativity 48, 198, 204
critical comment 94
cross discipline 135
culture 170
curiosity 56, 203
customer need 58

D
Design Thinking 89
dialogue 125
disruptive innovation 18
dual interdependency 166

E
Enterprise Resource Planning 177

evaluating radical innovation 126
evaluation 127
exploring 205

F

facilitator 37
facilitator tasks 38, 40, 44
far future solution 131
fast follower 32
first mover 32
framed search 86
framing 138
friction 94, 201, 203
Future Scenarios 125

G

gap analysis 132
Go extreme 67, 69

H

humor 55, 203

I

Iceberg Principle of Leadership 193
idea proposer 172
idea receiver 172
idea submission point 192
Imagination 201
implement 148
incentives 170
incentive system 173
incremental innovation 17
incremental solutions with a radical effect 124
in-depth knowledge 53
individual creativity 48
industrialization 21
innovation 20
innovation culture 182, 193

innovation pilot 197
innovation promotion system 175
inspiration 96
interdisciplinary group 197
invented here 166

J

justify in 61, 64, 138, 160
justify out 60, 64, 139, 160

L

late follower 32
LEAN 19
Lean Startup 50, 91, 140, 160
live performance 84

M

megatrends 96
mental anchor 131, 156
middle management 144
minimum viable product 108, 160
misconception 21
multiskill 46, 72, 102, 129

N

need-based innovation 58
need statement 130
Not Invented Here 159

O

openness 203
optimism 48, 49
outsource radical innovation 31

P

passive user 172
pioneering 135, 141
pioneers 86

Plug and Abandon 74
Polyphony 200
procession 135, 143
psychological safety 41, 54
pull 101
push 101

Q

quality assurance 184

R

radical group structure 111
radical innovation 18, 66
radical innovation network 111
radical solutions with an incremental effect 124
recognition 187
relational skill 54
respect 203
respectful 203
roadmap 132
role 95, 198, 204
room of opportunity 71, 202

S

scale up 107
Scenario Planning 125
scrapping ideas 94
S-curve 23
sea current power generator 112
second organizational structure 111
shared knowledge 201

Shepherd leadership 85
Showstoppers 91
silo 136, 143, 198, 205
silo work 129
social intelligence 54
strategy 120, 125
sustainable growth 170
systematic curiosity 102

T

test 44, 77, 89, 140
testing 68, 77, 185
timing 100

U

ultimate concept 161
understand the task 66

V

virtual team 37
visual 52
visualization 53

W

wide knowledge 53
workshop 128

Z

zoom out 62